*Cover: Galahad drawing the sword from the stone.
In: Lancelot-Grail: The Quest for the Holy Grail, (Queste del Saint-Graal), Cambrai or Saint-Omer-Thérouanne, 1290. Parchment, folio 405. Manuscript held in the Bibliothèque Nationale de France (BnF).*

© 2020, Virgile Pace

Published by: BoD - Books on Demand
12/14 rond-point des Champs-Élysées,
75008 Paris, France

Printed by: Books on Demand GmbH, Norderstedt, Germany

ISBN: 9782322260652

Legal Deposit: December 2020

First print run of 10 numbered copies on large-format vellum

Translated from the original French
"Le Graal et le golf – La Quête du golf inspiré"
by Elizabeth Guill

The illuminated letters were drawn ex gratia *by Clément Faure, a companion in the Quest, to whom I extend my warmest thanks.*

Virgile Pace

Golf and the Grail

The Quest for Inspired Golf

Preface by
Édouard Montaz

Acknowledgments

Special thanks to my wife Antonella, Henri-Pierre, my father, Claude, my friend, my brother, and companion in the quest, "chief" Patrick, thanks to whom this Adventure began, Jacques and Nicole, my grandparents, who introduced me to the Grail and who have now entered the Castle of the Fisher King. Your unfailing love and support nourished my quest for inspired golf.

To Shawn

Your "wisdom" leads the way to inspired golf. Your grateful children.

To Édouard

Cantor of inspired golf pedagogy. Without you, this book would not exist.

To my son, Joseph.

An inspired little golfer. With all my love. "Infinity times infinity plus infinity".

PREFACE

I will never forget my first meeting with Virgile in Paris, seven years ago when it all began.

He had contacted me several days previously. He was living in Italy, in Rome, at the time. He had just discovered my work and videos on YouTube and wanted to take lessons with me at any price, for "an entire week, every day for two hours." He would come to Paris for that express reason. It was "urgent". I was, he said, "his last chance".

He had tried everything. Every possible method imaginable. He had read everything. Seen everything. In vain. He was making no progress. Golf was merely a "source of physical and psychological suffering". He wanted to give up this "thankless" sport for "schizophrenics". This time, he swore, for good.

When I saw him for the first time, what struck me was the orange notebook he was carrying. A thick, laminated notebook. No pupil had ever before come to me for golf lessons in this fashion. I was intrigued.

I could not believe my eyes. In the notebook he had copied down everything I had said in all my videos. For the past ten years. To the letter. In meticulous detail. A monumental, incredible task. I was lost for words. My sense of connection with this extra-terrestrial hit me like a bolt of lightning and was reciprocated. It was obvious that I must never leave this extraordinary terrestrial being.

On the slopes of Etna, in the Roman Campagna, as far afield as Antananarivo and Malaza in Madagascar, Virgile became a 'quest' companion. For real. For better or for worse, as we say.

Never have I argued so much with a pupil. Never have I encountered so much resistance. Never have I had to draw so heavily and so extensively on my resources to find the 'right' analogies and the 'right' words.

And then, finally, after countless ordeals, misunderstandings and doubts, the miracle occurred.

This book gives an account of the long journey that is the lot of the apprentice golfer. It is told through his eyes and not those of the teacher, which makes it unique.

It is the pupil's book. My pupils, who are my teachers. But also my friends, because the inspired golf quest is above all a quest of friendship, fraternity, and love.

Édouard, 12 June 2020.

PROLOGUE

I.

THE SECRET OF THE GRAIL
AND THE QUEST FOR INSPIRED GOLF

Placing the quest for the Holy Grail[1] on a par with the search for inspired golf is undoubtedly somewhat risky. Blasphemous some might say. Detrimental, sacrilege. They are not altogether wrong.

Even if one was presumptuous enough to describe golf as an art, it is difficult, at first sight, to see anything other than those elements purely intrinsic to all sporting disciplines: training, preparation, practice, competition, and perfor-

---

[1] The remarkable calligraphy of the letter *noun*, the fourteenth in the Arab alphabet, brings to mind the Grail. The Spirit of God made manifest or the divine light, symbolised by the dot, fills the Holy Receptacle, or Man, represented by the symbol at the base of the letter.

mance. However, upon careful reflection, we might risk drawing a cautious parallel.

Firstly, because learning to play golf and the search for a truly authentic *swing*[2] are not by any means completely unlike the quest for the Grail and the adventures of the Round Table.

In particular, an analogy may be drawn between the initiation to the quest and the obstacle course encountered by the apprentice golfer.

The initiation to golf espouses, in fact, the major stages that characterise any quest: the long, hard road, discouragement linked to obscurantism, disappointment in the ordinary world, forces that hinder progress, the call to adventure, the meeting with the providential man, a guide who has himself been taught by a master, difficult at first and an object of confrontation, then the revelatory enlightenment that leads to knowledge and at last, the presence of, and communion and sharing with, the companions on the quest.

And secondly, because in the Quest for the Holy Grail, the most important thing is not the Grail itself, but the Quest. Not so much success, but rather "that ardent desire to surpass oneself

---
[2] Complete movement made with the club.

without which there is no great enterprise"³. The search for "adventure", as understood by the Medieval authors: the desire, not to experience the extraordinary and perform material exploits, but to sublimate everyday life, often disappointing in its repetition, through a spiritual journey where every action has meaning and becomes a sign, in order to arrive at the essential.

The essential. Or more accurately, the quintessential. The fifth corner of four. The total realisation of body, soul and Spirit that alone allows one to find the path that leads to the Holy City, the one that every Man carries within Himself.

---

[3] In : Xavier de Langlais : *Le roman du roi Arthur* (The Legend of King Arthur), volume V : *La fin des temps aventureux* (The End of Adventurous Times). Édition d'art H. Piazza, Paris, 19 November 1971.

II.

THE CASTLE OF THE GRAIL
AND CASTLES BUILT OF SAND

n the castle of the Fisher King, a strange citadel lost in the clouds, "so poorly defended and yet more inaccessible than all the fortified citadels in the world"[4], Perceval sees the Holy Grail appear. Dazzled by the beauty and radiance of the spectacle before him, he nonetheless remains locked in a guilty silence that hastens the disappearance of the strange procession and precious receptacle.

For the Christian, the Grail may symbolise many things: a holy vase that collected the blood of Christ on the cross, a cup used for

---

[4] In : Xavier de Langlais : *Le roman du roi Arthur*, op.cit. ; Volume III : *Aventures de Perceval et de Galaad* (*The Adventures of Perceval and Galahad*).

communion during the Last Supper, a basket filled with food that is continually renewed, a drinking horn whose nectar confers youth and joy, a cauldron of abundance that is a source of wisdom, a miraculous basket associated with the idea of sovereignty[5].

But the Grail extends to the universal. Stripped of its Latino-Greek filter, multiple in its forms yet one in its essence, it is at the heart of the other great spiritualities.

Jalāl ad-Dīn Muhammad Rūmī, a contemporary of Saint Francis of Assisi, founder in the 13th century of one of the greatest Muslim brotherhoods, the *Mevlevi* Order, and considered to be one of the greatest universal mystic poets, writes of "beauty unveiled, that reaches up out of the earth, as the sun appears in the Orient"[6].

The Arab influence on the legend of the Grail is no longer in doubt[7]. We now know that in the

---

[5]In : Danielle Quéruel, *Le Conte du Graal (The Story of the Grail)*, Temporary exhibition mounted by Thierry Delcourt, *La légende du roi Arthur (The Legend of King Arthur)*, Bibliothèque nationale de France, Paris, 2009.

[6]In : Jalāl ad-Dīn Muhammad Rūmī : *Mathnawî (3768 et ss.)*, translated from the Persian by Eva de Vitray Meyerovitch and Djamchid Mortazavi.

[7]In : Pierre Ponsoye: *L'Islam et le Graal, Études sur l'ésotérisme du Parzival de Wolfram von Eschenbach, (Islam and the Grail, Studies on the Esoterism of Wolfram von Eschenbach's Parzival)*, Arché Milano, 1976.

Middle Ages, Christianity and Islam were not only at war. Between their political and religious elites, "over and above the anathema and the battles, there was not only superficial dialogue and meetings, but real spiritual concurrence".[8]

For a long time, the legend of the Grail remained unknown in the Hebraic tradition. Judaic esoterism founded on the Torah and the Kabbalah nonetheless mentions the realisation in Man of the total, unconditional being, *Adam Kadmon*. Although the Grail is a Revelation, it could also designate "the universal source of Being, [...] the unity that is the foundation of existence, *Élohim*, [...] the creative power, ineffable, transcendent".[9]

"I reach towards your light,
Cup, cup of crystal,
Buried within the rock of the soul",
wrote André Chouraqui in his *Cantique pour Nathanaël*, a poem inspired by a scholar who had succeeded in moving from the particular – Judaism – to the universal.[10]

---

[8]ibid.
[9]In : André Chouraqui : *Traduire les Textes sacrés, Trois Textes une tradition commune (Translating Sacred Texts, Three Texts, a Common Tradition)*, Centre audiovisuel de Paris, Arts et Éducation, April 1995.
[10]In : André Chouraqui : *Cantique pour Nathanaël*, Espaces libres, Albin Michel, Paris, 1991.

Astonishingly, visions of the Grail in the three great monotheistic religions are not unlike the teachings offered by the great Eastern spiritualities on attaining the Divine. The latter doubtless use different terminology, but the realities they describe evoke the God, or Principle, or transcendent state that bathes the universe and lives in the immanence of human hearts and minds.

How could it be otherwise? Monotheist religions say, "there is but one God". Eastern religions proclaim, "the gods are but one". Between these two affirmations, the abyss is colossal. The frontier tenuous.

Taoism invites Man to return to natural and primordial authenticity, to free himself from constraints and allow the spirit to "sit astride the clouds". Hinduism exalts the *Brahman*, the invisible, eternal, uncreated and infinite principle. Man must rediscover the divine primitive vibration of the universe that represents all existence, embracing all nature in an ultimate truth: "*Om*".

Buddhism aims to release Man from the *samsara*, the cycle of rebirth and the whirlwind of passions, through enlightenment and a state of mindfulness, which should lead to the end of *dukkha* – dissatisfaction – and *nirvana* – total deliverance.

Shintoism proclaims that Man is an element of the Great All. He must learn to live in harmony with the forces of the universe, the *kami*, and in communion with past generations through respect for his ancestors.

But what does this mean for the golfer? What is the Grail? How can it be reached? And above all, how can it be made a reality and not merely a hope, or even a vision? Because any vision, sweet and beautiful as it may be, is necessarily fleeting, slealthy, and destined to fade and disappear, like the painful episode experienced by Perceval.

For a long time, these questions obsessed me. And for a long time, they remained unanswered. Indeed, replying to them involves deep introspection that leads to another fundamental question: what is the true essence of golf?

Omitting this phase of questioning and self-examination is to take the risk of never glimpsing the Castle of the Grail and building castles made of sand that by their very definition are fragile, fleeting and destined to disappear as soon as the tide comes in, since they are motivated by superfluous considerations and built on imperfect, defective and incomplete foundations.

To simply try to send a little white ball as far as possible, to try merely to increase distance, to try mechanically to reproduce the same movement, to try, invariably, to acquire key techniques, to try obsessively to reproduce and imitate the swing of the greatest players: for a long time my quest was vain, my golf, a living hell.

Such aspirations are the preserve of golf that is controlled and technical and which favours solely the physical aspect and it took me many years to understand that they are the polar opposite of inspired golf because they lead to a preference for the superfluous rather than the essential, the fleeting rather than the imperishable, and the material rather than the spiritual dimension. They lead to a renouncement of all the intuitive, invisible, unintelligible elements of one's being.

To set out on such a path is therefore to set out on a meaningless quest, an unnatural quest in the true sense of the term since it does not take into account human *nature* in all its wholeness and with all its limitations. As a result, these aspirations lead to embarking on a dangerous path, strewn with pitfalls.

It is a path that leads to total errors and suffering coupled with enormous disappointment.

For a long time, learning golf was a long hard road.

PART ONE

INITIATION (CONSCIOUSNESS)

"Everyone is right from their own point of view, but it is not impossible that everyone is wrong".

MAHATMA GANDHI

III.

THE LONG HARD ROAD

"It is not the path that is the difficulty, but the difficulty that is the path". The Danish philosopher Sören Kierkegaard has a warning for the apprentice golfer of the difficulties and torments that lie ahead.

They are a necessary and inevitable passage to salvation, an educational, and not a destructive, force. They instruct, prepare, and guide the apprentice golfer throughout his long journey. Because golf may, for a long while, remain indecipherable and incomprehensible.

Insurmountable obstacles very quickly appeared before me. Gigantic ordeals lay in wait for me. Immense disappointments were in store for me.

Inspired golf appears at first to be an insoluble enigma.

The discovery of the limits inherent in all methods and to all teaching, in whatever form, was the first great disillusion I had to face and with it, the slow realisation, difficult to accept, that technical knowledge was not enough. Because a rule emerges that brooks no exception and which often brings bitterness and sorrow: work, practice, and the repetition of physical and technical exercises, however advanced, never suffice.

Hitting hundreds of balls in the driving range[11] every day, thousands every week, taking endless private and group lessons, trying every possible type of teacher, testing an incalculable number of methods, learning from hundreds of videos on the Net and as many books, is, in the quest for inspired golf, unproductive and vain.

If further proof is needed that the practice of golf cannot be reduced to an activity that can be mastered through practice, one need only heed the simple lamentation, disturbing yet recurrent amongst apprentice golfers, "the more I practice, the worse I play".

---

[11] In golf clubs, the area set aside for practice.

Inspired golf is first and foremost an exploration of the self. It can only be found within a player and not outside of him. Not only, at least.

Trying to understand golf solely from the outside, is to hit a brick wall, to collide with something impenetrable. This was the second great danger that lay in wait for me.

It took me a long time to understand that I must rid myself of all ambition and desire; the desire to do well, play better, be more successful, the desire to lower my handicap when my real handicap was 'I'.

"The right art is purposeless, aimless"[12].

Thinking, wishing, desiring, striving, hoping, calculating, planning: all these actions separated and distracted me from my quest.

Disappointed, discouraged, disillusioned and overcome by an indescribable lassitude, I raged, fulminated, lost my temper, and ranted and raved. Like Girflet, ordered by the dying King Arthur to throw *Excalibur* into a lake near Salisbury Plain where he had just fought his last battle, I too, twice tried to donate all my equipment to the Lady of the Lake. My fourteen blades were of no use to me. Robbed of all

---

[12]In : Eugen Herrigel : *Le zen dans l'art chevaleresque du tir à l'arc (Zen in the Art of Archery)*, Éditions Dervy, Paris, 1970.

magic power, they inevitably led me to defeat. Inexorably, implacably.

In his admirable work published in 1911, Arnaud Massy, world golf champion in 1907, wrote, "Little by little [...] a healthy diversion suspends their continual anxiety. Their aggressive, frantic nerves subside; without emotion or pain, their astonished muscles become more flexible. After the physical being, the moral being takes over and a benevolent peace brings them at last the much sought-after repose the sweetness of which had eluded them"[13]. Nothing could have been further from my state of mind.

Abandon, capitulate, give up. These words obsessed me, were constantly resounding in my brain.

All these words, all this pain.

---

[13]In : Arnaud Massy, *Le golf*, Sports-Bibliothèque, Pierre Lafitte et Cie, Paris, 1911.

IV.

OBSCURANTISM

Even today, the Middle Ages are still considered by many to be a period of obscurantism and regression in comparison with the two periods of enlightenment: Antiquity and the Renaissance. This is a mistake for two reasons.

Firstly, it is to forget that the Middle Ages saw the progressive constitution of the modern State thanks to the growth of public administration and codification of the laws, as well as the birth of the University, which contributed to giving the biggest towns "the impetus of learning, reasoning and the development of the sciences"[14].

---

[14] In : Séverine Boullay : *Le Moyen Âge : Temps obscurs ou siècles d'innovation ? (The Middle Ages : Dark Ages or Centuries of Innovation ?)* Lecture given on 7 October

Secondly, it is to forget that light does not exist without darkness and that chaos necessarily precedes order. "Like the water-lily, whitest of all, that plunges its roots into the sludge of dead waters"[15].

Obscurantism, and its corollary, ignorance, the *absence of knowledge* or *non-knowledge* therefore constitutes a necessary stage in the advancement towards knowledge. They prepare for it and prefigure it. Because ignorance leads to confusion. And confusion, to despair, the reaction to which creates the desire for something else. And above all, the desire for a future.

After fifteen unsuccessful golfing years, I felt this desire growing within myself. The golf of postures and key techniques, that of the camera and technologies, no longer suited me. Sequential, rational golf that attempted to explain everything scientifically and analyse everything in minute detail, was preventing me from making progress.

Finally, I had to admit it. I had wandered from the path. I systematically associated distance with control and effort, without trying other

---

2017 during the *Rendez-vous de l'Histoire de Blois,* Bibliothèque nationale de France.
[15]In: Xavier de Langlais, *Le roman du roi Arthur,* op.cit., Volume III.

ways. I spent hours, often in front of a mirror, trying to find the correct spatial placement of the club for the backswing[16]. Never with a target. I had a thousand pieces of information circulating in my head as I lifted my club, but without ever linking them to a sensation.

Remain completely focused, leaning on my left side. Remain firmly anchored with both feet placed solidly on the ground, come up in a line, almost outside, in order to be completely vertical. Lengthen my arms to gain width. Slow down my upswing to be able to accelerate on the way down. Finish my movement correctly, remembering to turn my shoulders. And all this without excessive tension, to encourage me to relax my grip[17] and the pressure of my hands on the club.

Each time, with each stroke, I tried in vain to put all this into practice. I had made thousands of summaries with well-chosen keywords, intended to help me, or so I thought, to simplify all these tasks and above all, to assist my brain during the few crucial fractions of a second upon which all depended.

"*Nothing* - no tension -, *Y* - action consisting in placing the shaft[18] in front of the head of the

---

[16]Backward movement of the swing beginning on the ground and finishing above the head.
[17]Manner of holding the club.
[18]Literally "handle". This is the shaft of the club.

club - *click* - an action consisting in bending the left knee to the front when beginning the *swing* -, *outside, shoulder/shoulder*". And I hit a slice[19]. « *Nothing, Y, chantilly* - an image intended to help me apply truly light hand pressure -, *click, squat*[20], *outside, turn* ». And I hit a *hook*[21]. "*Nothing, Y, chantilly, click, squat, outside, slow down, shoulder/shoulder, accelerate, turn*". And I hit a fat shot[22].

The more I thought, the more I analysed, the more I controlled, the less I succeeded in playing golf. It was incredible. Deeply unfair. But there was an implacable mathematical logic to it: my results were in reverse proportion to my efforts and my work.

Surely there was a rational explanation. I was missing something, that was clear. But what?

I was confused, disoriented, drowning in a sea of often contradictory information and detail. The confusion I was feeling showed in my game. I was incapable of consistency. And I could not explain why, in the space of several

---

[19] A missed shot that causes the ball to follow a trajectory with an exaggerated curve to the right.
[20] Bending of the legs during the *downswing* to gain power from the ground.
[21] A miss-hit where the trajectory curves markedly to the left.
[22] A miss-hit consisting of touching the ground before the ball.

seconds, I could hit a fantastic shot followed by another that was catastrophic.

In addition to all this, this type of golf with its supposedly technically perfect movement that could be reproduced an infinite number of times, only served to cause me pain and injuries, particularly in my neck, back and knee. Anti-inflammatories, heat packs, homeopathic remedies and balms of all kinds, in particular Devil's Claw *(sic)*, accompanied me in my apprenticeship of golf.

This methodical, Cartesian golf, known for its certainties, was for me the golf of disillusion. Strangely, it gave rise in me only to doubts and questions. What if this was the golf of the blind leading the blind? The golf of obscurantism?

I now had a deep-seated conviction that there must be another sort of golf, a type of golf based on a better understanding of Man and the environment and therefore able to put an end to all my physical and psychological trauma. Golf that was holistic and not sequential, capable of reconciling opposites, technique and sensation, and therefore capable of solving all the contradictions and all the improbabilities of traditional teaching, true pedagogy and not yet another method, attentive to the pupils and their difficulties, and therefore able to perfect tools, images and tasks indefinitely. The golf of the enlightenment or more precisely, a golf able to increase the potential for shedding light on the matter to enlighten the golfer.

    Illuminating the matter, transforming it, in the spirit of the assumption. The great work of the alchemists, the initiates of the Middle Ages.

V.

DISAPPOINTMENT IN THE EVERYDAY WORLD

In the apprenticeship of golf, the most common approach consists in making the discipline difficult, excessively complicated and almost inaccessible. As a result, it is an approach that is often the expression of a seizure of power and based on deceit.

Seizure of power: that of teachers over pupils so as to retain the preserve of the teaching of golf and from the top of their pedestal, to make the transmission and acquisition of their knowledge excessively slow and long, sometimes for mercantile ends.

Deceit: by inciting the apprentice golfer to reproduce a movement that is supposedly perfect for all, by encouraging him to imitate the swing of the world's top players, these teachers forget to specify that the physical and biophysical qualities of amateur players are not, and cannot be, those of professional players or high-level sportsmen and women.

The world of the amateur is not that of the professional. As a result, disappointment is inevitable. Understanding that expectations have not been met, that the miracle has not occurred, is painful.

My disappointment was not "metaphysical" in the manner of Stendhal's heroes when they realise that the possession of the "thing" has not changed their being, that "the expected metamorphosis has not happened"[23]. It really was palpable, tangible, and objective. Nothing and nobody could help me. I was running on the spot, making no further progress despite my efforts. My sacrifices had brought about no transfiguration or emancipation and no liberation.

The result was a deep-rooted feeling of failure. And Emptiness. Once again, I had the feeling I was on the edge of the abyss.

I was wrong. I later understood that disappointment is an unavoidable stage in any learn-

---

[23] In : René Girard : *Mensonge romantique et vérité romanesque (Deceit, Desire and the Novel : Self and Other in Literary Structure)*, Éditions Grasset et Fasquelle, Paris, 1961.

ing process. It is an integral part of the quest, in the same way as King Arthur's companions had to experience the harsh existence of the knight errant, "richer in sorrow than honours"[24], before they could take part in the search for the Holy Grail. This was particularly true of Perceval, son of Gamuret and Herzeloid, the champion in Vermillion Arms, with the "simple and pure heart"[25], whose sins, doubts and disappointments condemned him to long years of wandering and oblivion.

But only for a time. Because "our senses teach us that every night, long as it may be, must come to an end"[26].

---

[24]In: Xavier de Langlais: *Le roman du roi Arthur*, op.cit., volume III.
[25]ibid.
[26]ibid.

VI.

FORCES THAT DELAY PROGRESS

he Archangel Saint Michael, guardian of the flaming sword, triumphant over Hell, floored the dragon, symbol of the forces that delay the awakening to the light of true knowledge. Yet he did not kill it. He fought and tamed it.

When I first began, prey to a thousand doubts and a thousand questions, I too had to tame my inner demons, not to completely eradicate them, but to transfigure them, thanks to an appropriate apprenticeship.

It was a delicate task. Thorns and invading, distracting forces proliferate within us all. For a long time, false hopes, illusory expectations, inappropriate training sessions, and the improper use of clubs delayed my progress, turning me away from what I was really searching for: authenticity.

False hopes.

Like many amateur golfers, to gain distance and drive[27] a long way was my greatest ambition. It brought me nothing but sorrow and affliction.

The truth is that practice is not enough. Neither on the driving range nor in the gym. The morphology of the body, its constitution, the nature of its tissues and muscular fibre, fast or not, are the true determinants of distance. Age too, plays a discriminatory role in measurement and distance in golf, requiring a flexibility and muscular tonus that is more difficult to acquire or develop as the years pass.

Illusory expectations.

The search for a "good" score and its corollary, an improvement in the index[28] was my greatest ambition. Alas! This is inevitably destined to fail. And lead to great dissatisfaction.

It is a mistake on two counts. On the one hand, it turns the index into an exact barometer of the player's level in the game, which is inac-

---

[27]Describes a shot played with the *driver*, still called wood number 1. The *drive* is generally played from the tee-box with the ball placed on a tee and is intended to send the ball a long way.
[28]The *index* is the player's official ranking.

curate. The index can be deceptive: it favours players who play numerous competitions, those who play on easy courses and those who cheat. It also takes little account of the effective quality of the game played. One can, for example, shoot a *bogey*[29] after a perfect tee-shot, a beautiful approach at more than a hundred and twenty metres from the flag on a long, difficult *green*[30] with a double plateau, and a first, remarkable *putt*[31] that sends the ball almost a metre from the hole, but then miss the last *putt* by a few millimetres. One mediocre shot will have been enough to ruin three perfectly executed shots.

On the other hand, it is possible to play a *birdie* after sending a tee-shot into the trees because of a slight *slice*, *topping*[32] the ball on the second centring despite which it manages to roll right up to the green, and hit a long *putt*, played too hastily, without preparation and with an inadequate preparatory routine. The quality of the shots executed would doubtless be much inferior to that of those described in the previous example. The result would, however, be

---

[29] Hole played one stroke above *par*. *Double Bogey*: two strokes above *par*. *Triple bogey* etc.
[30] Area of closely trimmed grass around the hole, marked by a flag.
[31] Shot played on the green with a *putter*.
[32] Making contact with the ball above or on its equator.

better in terms of score. An exclusively numerical approach cannot therefore be satisfying.

Moreover, it should not be forgotten that the apprentice golfer does not possess the arms that would allow him to overcome all the obstacles and pitfalls of the course.

If he is to be an effective player, he must, in fact, master at least seven major types of stroke: the tee-shot, progression strokes, attacking the green, pitching[33], rolled and lifted approaches, the bunkers[34] on the course and those situated near the greens, and lastly the putts.

In addition, each of these major categories require the player to cope with an infinite number of variants, to know how to adapt to a myriad of variables depending on the slopes, lies[35], qualities of the fairways[36], roughs[37], configuration of the hole, the obstacles, the out-of-bounds, and weather conditions.

The series of shots that need to be mastered is always enormous. Practising once or twice a week, even in the best of cases, is not enough.

---

[33]Approach shot played high with a pitching wedge.
[34]Hollow obstacle filled with sand, placed on a fairway or around the green.
[35]Way in which the ball rests on the ground.
[36]Mown part of the course, between the tee and the green, supposed to be the ideal playing area.
[37]Area of high grass.

Moe Norman, the Canadian prodigy was amongst the first to warn the apprentice golfer against an obsession with the score. He recommended that one should, in all circumstances, armed with playing expertise and experience, adopt an *"alert attitude of indifference"*[38]: remaining ever "alert" to the choices to be made and to the "correct" prediction, in complete indifference to the result. Not because it did not matter but precisely because the best means of achieving a satisfactory card is by not trying to. The apprentice golfer cannot be master of the score. What is important is the way in which it is "built up".

Inappropriate training sessions.

In golf, some consider that the more one practices, the more one progresses. Mechanically. Symmetrically. Nothing could be further from the truth. Consequently, I quickly became aware of two things.

On the one hand, it is not enough to train hard to have immediate results. Taking the results of the work done on the driving range onto the course is not automatic, far from it.

There is one main reason for this: driving ranges do not reproduce, or very imperfectly, actual playing conditions.

---

[38] Attitude of increased vigilance.

Chalking up endless drives and woods, playing an increasing number of shots with hybrid clubs or irons, always under the same conditions, with the same posture, is of limited interest.

And yet at the same time, I did not devote enough time to practice. Ideally, I should have been practising putting half the time. I was supposed, in fact, to execute a total of seventy-two shots, to include thirty-six putts, that is, half the number of shots expected on a course. This was far from being the case.

Similarly, I too often neglected the short game, and approach and recovery shots[39]. Moreover, before playing each shot, I did not always take care to choose a target, determine the trajectory of the ball and the corresponding spin, to find the appropriate position or the appropriate sensation, that which corresponded to the image.

The improper use of the clubs at my disposal also hindered my progress for a long time. The use of the fourteen clubs authorised by the rules of golf was a formidable trap. For at least two reasons.

---

[39]This is a re-centring shot, generally played on an uneven or difficult section of the course, to come back onto the fairway or, in the best of cases, to arrive on the green.

Firstly, because I could not control all the clubs, which led me to "force" my shots, preventing "relaxed" play.

Secondly, because it encouraged me to make the wrong choices in terms of strategy.

Later on, whenever I forced myself to limit the number of clubs I used (usually five: a putter[40], a sand wedge[41], a nine iron, a seven iron, and a five iron), I played significantly better. A more restrained use of clubs had obliged me to ask myself fewer questions, be more indulgent with myself, pay greater attention to strategy, be more responsive to my environment and to be more creative. A seven-iron allowed me to play an incredible variety of shots, from a chipping shot to a putt.

Like the quest for the Grail, the search for inspired golf may be likened to "climbing a vertiginous staircase cut into a rockface next to an abyss"[42]. At each stage, or even each step, I had to fight against the fear of the shadows and the pull of the vacuum. In other words, against myself.

---

[40]Club, the loft of which is between 2 and 6° and which is used in putting.
[41]Club used to get the ball out of the sand.
[42]In : Xavier de Langlais, *Le Roman du roi Arthur*, op.cit. ; Volume IV : *La Quête du Graal*.

VII.

THE SEARCH FOR "ADVENTURE"

In the stories of the Round Table, Adventure allows the knight errant to demonstrate his courage, valour and skill in the art of war. It is also an opportunity to test his faith and virtue. Adventure is at the heart of the quest for the Grail. When it was slow in presenting itself at Arthur's court, the court became "morose and paralysed and lost its dynamism and strength"[43]. Indeed, progress was only achieved through adventure. Testing proved valour. But not only.

---

[43] In : Danielle Quéruel, *Le chevalier errant et l'Aventure*, Exposition temporaire réalisée par Thierry Delcourt, *La légende du roi Arthur* (*The knight errant and Adventure. Temporary exhibition mounted by Thierry Delcourt, The Legend of King Arthur*), op. cit.

A true "hero at arms and love"[44], ready to continually place himself in danger, the knight set off on a quest for his own identity. Adventure is, above all, a search for identity. The knights had to discover their true nature and accomplish, or invent, their own destiny. Off the beaten track.

Lost in the meanders of mechanical golf, for a long time I felt the same as the knights errant. I was making no further progress and was looking for something different. I had the feeling that golf was far more than a "pleasant pastime", yet I could not manage to find this other reality. I felt like Calogrenant, at the beginning of *Yvain, le Chevalier au Lion (Yvain, the Knight of the Lion)*, who answers the peasant who asks him who he is, saying *"I am a knight searching for what cannot be found. My search has lasted a long time and yet has remained vain"* [45].

Conscious of having taken a wrong turning, I was nevertheless ready to pursue my great "adventurous" search, an intuitive, not systematic search that has neither principle nor method, a search for authenticity, beauty, and perfection.

---

[44]ibid.
[45]In : Chrétien de Troyes, *Yvain, le Chevalier au Lion (Yvain, the Knight of the Lion),* written around 1176.

Authenticity that aims to exalt the greatness, rectitude, and honour within each and every one of us.

Beauty, the true aesthetic experience in the Medieval sense of the word[46], the purpose of which is to enhance the virtue of the soul. The physical beauty, of Blancheflor, Guinevere, Igraine, Iseult, Fenice, Laudine, Enide, and Soredamor that inspires love in the knights and incites them to constantly surpass themselves and accept tests and suffering that they may be worthy of the esteem of their ladies, sacred figures at one and the same time muses and sources of inspiration. The metaphysical beauty, that is issue of the divine ideal, the "conjunction of moral, spiritual intellectual and possibly sensorial elements that between them form a manner of perfection"[47].

---

[46]The aesthetic is understood as a meta-aesthetic *"a philosophy of sensory experience that does not systematically treat its subject separately as an object of knowledge or episteme, but includes it within a wider area of various orders of questions, the ontological, religious and ethical and their derivatives"* In: Valérie Gonzalez, *Le beau et l'expérience esthétique dans la pensée musulmane du Moyen Âge*, Le beau et le laid au Moyen Âge *(Beauty and the Aesthetic Experience,* Beauty and Ugliness in the Middle Ages) Presses Universitaires de Provence, Aix-en-Provence, 2000.
[47]ibid.

Perfection, which is plenitude and harmony and a constant invitation to push back the limits of what is possible. The golf ball, as it slows down, describes two circles in the shape of an "8". This "8" symbolises infinity, without end. Infinity, by definition, remains unexplored.

For me, the quest for inspired golf became the greatest Adventure there is. As a result, it was shrouded in mystery.

The Valley of No Return, "path of mad thought", Fountain of Barenton, Tom Thumb, the Castle of Dolorous Gard, Castle of Maidens, the Meadow, the Adventurous Citadel, manor of images, bridge of the secret, iron-clad angels, the woman in rags, desecrated tomb, abandoned oratory, poisoned fruit, Carteloise Castle, boat of the dead maiden, test of the broken sword; it is only after innumerable adventures and tests that the Grail finally appears.

The miracle almost always happens thanks to intervention by a spiritual guide, a real *deus ex machina* sent by Providence, the "divine law that travels *incognito*", and without which the quest is doomed to failure.

VIII.

THE PROVIDENTIAL MAN

My meeting with my guide did not happen in the heart of a dense forest, by an enchanted fountain nor amidst a thick mist. Yet it was nonetheless epic. It was the meeting of two strong, quixotic, fully rounded personalities who made no concessions.

Édouard had long been convinced that success was inevitable, sure of the pedagogy of Shawn, the great master who had knighted him several years earlier and who had tasked him with disseminating his work in Europe, his philosophy in the literal sense of the term being: the love of wisdom, *wisdom in golf*.

For my part, I, on the other hand, was persuaded that golf could bring the apprentice golfer nothing but suffering, frustration and tears and I was now convinced that no teaching or teacher could be of any use to me. Our meeting therefore quickly became one of confrontation and opposition.

Ours was soon a dialogue of the deaf between two unreconcilable extremes: on the one hand the unbelievable talent of a gifted man who had made the search for inspired golf his profession and on the other, the disillusionment of an amateur who had lost all hope of improving and remained resolutely unamenable to any teaching.

The heat of the confrontation that established itself between us was fierce. Extremely fierce. Our discussions resembled those of two duellists engaged in a fight to the death rather than those of teacher and pupil.

Almost despite ourselves, we discovered that the higher the expectations and the greater the affliction, the slower and more painful, the apprenticeship. Discouragement, lost temper, abandonment, and tension were, in the beginning, extreme. We did not know at the time that this was a condition of future success. Because this being so, it gave full meaning to the word "Quest", which cannot exist, in fact, unless the point of non-return has been reached.

Unless, at a given moment, all hope has been lost.

IX.

THE VERBAL JOUST

As in the beginning of the Middle Ages, or later, from the 13th century onwards, during tournaments when jousts between two knights on horseback armed with a lance galloped towards each other, the verbal clash between us was extremely vehement.

During my first lessons, still reluctant to admit any change and battling my old demons, I persistently took an opposing stance to Édouard over every piece of advice he offered me, objecting to each of his analogies, rejecting all his messages, contradicting all his images.

"The Elephant Walk", therefore became "the Graveyard of the Elephants", "perpetual motion[48]", "perpetual regrets", "the three swings [rhythmic golf]", "the three nothings" [arrhythmic golf]", "the lag in the golf swing", "my golf swing is lagging", "success is inevitable", "chronicle of a death foretold", and "self-preservation", "self-destruction".

Nothing could stop me. I doubled my efforts and became ever more imaginative.

"The [correct] posture", became "the imposture",
"catapult", "cataplasm", "tilted spiral", "negative spiral", "the right command", "my body no longer obeys", "moving the body out of the way", "playing truant", "re-invent [each stroke]", "reproduce [the same movement]", "prediction", "eviction", "prepare yourself for the right collision", "straight into the wall", and "gravity [abandoning control]", "my gravity [my arms are falling off]".

---

[48]Perpetual motion is a key element of Shawn and Édouard's pedagogy. To do this, the player should swing the arm-club unit, back and forth without stopping, from right to left like a pendulum. Perpetual motion can only be perfectly executed if the arms never come into contact with the chest. This is only possible if the body "moves completely out of the way" of the two sides of the swing. The rotation of the body is in harmony with the sensation of the weight of the arm-club unit in movement.

I pushed Édouard up against the wall. I was constantly provoking him.

"Power comes from the ground up" became "six feet under", "throw *the* clubs" {towards the target], "throw away *my* clubs", "gardener [whipping the grass]", "wild boar [uprooting the grass]", "carpenter [the door frame]", "ragman [the door that slams]", and "another bone [arm-club united]", "a bone to pick [arm-club disjointed]".

Édouard stood his ground, though not without difficulty. I returned to the charge, forcing him to constantly find new images and tasks, pushing him into a corner. I had suffered too much. I wanted to be certain. Certain I could place my trust in him.

"Centrifugal force" became "the centrifuge", "the release of energy[49]", "energy born of desperation", "letting go", ready to "let it all go", "sentiment", a "feeling of resentment", "sand pit [Child's game]", "learning to live in the 'bunker' [War game]", "on a downward path", "on a slippery slope", "*eau non*! [Carpe diem]", "oh no! [Empathy with carp]", "the beauty of the *fade*"[50], "my golf is fading away", "the beauty of the

---

[49]Literally, "liberation".
[50]Trajectory of the ball from left to right, for a right-handed player.

draw" [51], "*draw* is *draw*"! and "Observation: recognizing the golf course", "exploration: the call of the wild".

Whether on the *driving range*, or on the *fairways*, my impression was always the same: we were re-writing the adventures of the two characters created by William Hanna and Joseph Barbara: Édouard and Virgile, or rather Dastardly and Muttley[52], playing golf. There was just one difference. Any happy ending was proscribed. When Dastardly spoke of "a good finish[53], Muttley concluded it was "game over"!

Golf and anti-golf? Not so sure.

As our confrontation continued a strange complicity grew up between us, a strange alchemy, as though we were moved by a similar force, animated by a common intention, turned towards the same goal. And what if inspired golf could only be found at the crossroads of these paths, of these destinies? In the place where absolute joy meets extreme suffering, ecstasy meets torment and the self-evident encounters the most appalling doubts.

---

[51] Trajectory of the ball from right to left for a right-handed player.
[52] William Hanna and Joseph Barbara: *Dastardly and Muttley in Their Flying Machines*, American cartoon broadcast for the first time in 1969 by CBS.
[53] Position of the golfer at the end of a swing.

X.

KNIGHTHOOD

All disciples, before they become guides themselves, are taught by a master. In the Arthurian literature and the cycle of the Grail, the young princes and lords, or unknown people whom we supposed to be of noble lineage, have but one ambition: to go to Arthur's court to be knighted. Being knighted by the king is a real initiation ritual, a rite of passage that will allow them to become part of the 'egalitarian' family of the Knights of the Round Table.

To be knighted is worthy of recognition. It is a supreme honour, but also an immense responsibility. The knight must not only demonstrate unshakeable loyalty and faithfulness, but charged with a supreme mission, he is also continually obliged to show his valour and value through combat and his search for adventures.

Édouard was not knighted on the soil of Brittany or Great Britain, but on that of Canada, not far from Toronto. In the *Richmond Hill Golf Learning Center*.

When he saw Édouard execute his first perpetual motions, Shawn Clement recognised him immediately. A magnificent interpreter of the choreography he had created several years earlier, and which constituted the essence of his new pedagogy, Édouard was literally dancing before his eyes. He swung the club back and forth admirably, without stopping, cutting the grass on both sides of the arc of the swing.

All was harmony and melody. A sublime natural setting added to the magic of the moment. One could almost hear an old Mississauga chief humming the words of the famous song, *Indian Summer*:

"It was Autumn, a beautiful Autumn. A season that only exists in North America. Over there they call it Indian Summer"[54].

On that October day in the year of our Lord two thousand and nine, Shawn understood that without knowing it, he had always been waiting for Édouard.

---

[54]In : Joe Dassin : *Indian Summer*, a song co-written by Pierre Delanoë and Claude Lemesle, CBS, 1975.

Édouard, whom so many trials, and so much work and thought had finally led to Shawn.

Against all odds.

Édouard, the brilliant disciple, the child prodigy.

XI.

THE VISIONARY TROUBADOUR

Shawn likes to say that he came into the world to help people improve their golf and above all, to enjoy it. He is convinced that golf is within the reach of anybody and that success is inevitable, provided one concentrates on the "right tasks".

At the age of seventeen, Shawn joined the Canadian Ski Patrol. It was a tough experience that allowed him to acquire a thorough knowledge of the human body since he had not only to learn life-saving techniques to help injured companions in the hostile environment of the high Canadian mountains, but also to relay highly accurate and comprehensive information to the hospital doctors to facilitate their emergency response.

Shawn possesses several unique characteristics. To date, he is, for example, the only professional player to have played in the Canadian Tour as both a right and left-handed player. Half the clubs in his bag were right-handed and half, left-handed.

Very quickly however, Shawn realised that his greatest ambition was not to play on the professional circuits. His vocation lay elsewhere. Sharing his passion, transmitting his knowledge, demonstrating his experience and expertise in golf gave meaning to his life.

Armed with his knowledge of human anatomy, he then embarked on a novel undertaking. He decided to analyse all the existing methods of teaching golf, study them and extract the best.

In doing so, he made a surprising and disturbing observation. All, without exception, worked in opposition to the human body and brain in that they ignored the way in which it worked and its fundamental mechanisms. Not only did they discount the natural mobility of the human body, advocating on the contrary, the resistance of the lower body in the backswing - known as the *X factor* - but they also disregarded the most elementary laws of physics, first of which was gravity, favouring only static and isometric swing positions. All this condemns the apprentice golfer to permanently manipulating his swing, causing repeated injuries, particularly to the back.

Shawn therefore decided to remedy what he considered to be an error. Little by little, he perfected a pedagogy based on total respect for the human anatomy and on an understanding of the way the brain functions. To do this, he studied the work of the greatest neurologists and specialists in human behaviour. This led him to develop his whole analysis of the 'right' commands and the 'right' tasks: aiming for a target, visualising an image, cutting the grass, releasing[55] to the right or to the left of an intermediate focal point, 'throwing' a club.

One of Shawn's great merits lies in having found accessible words and elementary analogies to translate and explain the morphology, neurology, psychology, physiology and the physique of the human body as well as the environment and physical laws that govern our planet Earth.

Making the complicated simple. This is real pedagogy. Useful pedagogy.

A balanced posture and complete rotation of the hips and thoracic cage, thanks to respect for the body, energy dispensed effortlessly, thanks

---

[55] Describes the fact of delivering, liberating an action towards a target.

to the laws of physics, response to an external and dynamic *focus* command, thanks to an understanding of the brain: Shawn had pierced the secret of a golf that was finally achievable by everyone.

Learning to delegate rather than control. Learning to abandon rather than manipulate. Learning to feel, rather than to analyse. Shawn's wisdom has transformed the amateur golfer for ever, imposing a new vision of the human being on a golf course.

Vitruvian Man. Man of Vicissitudes no longer.

Shawn is a troubadour. He is, quite literally, a *trouveur,* a 'finder'.

He who has found the light and who shows the way. He who has opened up the path to inspired golf.

XII.

INITIATION

Unlearning. Paradoxically, this is the aim of any initiation. It was the first lesson that Édouard gave me. The apprenticeship of inspired golf begins with a break. Contrary to current teaching that usually tries to construct swings through resistance, traumatising the body and causing repeated injuries, it is based on total respect for the human body.

Contrary to methods based on the use of the camera and images, which attempt to shape the apprentice golfer in a prefabricated mould, inviting him to reproduce the swing of the greatest players in the world, inspired golf encourages the expression of a swing that is unique to each player.

Contrary to the tools that teach a sequential approach leading to the development of a robotic swing[56], it favours a holistic approach that takes account of the environment and highlights appropriate tasks that allow the body to move effortlessly.

Contrary to approaches that lead to manipulating the body and the club in the illusory hope of acquiring total domination and infallible control of the swing, it encourages letting go and abandoning control.

Contrary to ceaselessly reminding the apprentice golfer that his swing is defective and in permanent need of repair, placing him in the worst possible state of mind, "the state of hope and fear" – the hope of success and the fear of failure – it emphasises that the swing is above all natural and must be left to express itself naturally, in an almost unconscious manner.

This was the second great lesson that Édouard taught me: inspired golf is the expression of a realisation and reveals a hidden truth.

---

[56] All the sequences of the golf swing are first isolated, analysed and worked on separately before being placed end to end. They are then supposed to constitute a perfect golf swing: address, takeaway, half backswing, top of the backswing, transition, balance recovery, release, follow-through (post-impact stage of the swing that accompanies the ball before the finish itself), and the finish.

The realisation that learning to play golf does not consist so much in 'constructing' one's own swing in accordance with one's own attributes, but rather in 'rediscovering' a treasure hidden deep within and exalting it through simple principles, anchored in each of us.

The hidden truth that to deliver an action towards a target, throw a projectile, create speed without excessive tension, each apprentice golfer, for each of these actions, has the benefit of an expertise that goes back millions of years, an expertise passed down to him by the hunter-gatherers of the Paleolithic era, almost two million and a half years ago. Consequently, the cinematic sequence of acceleration characterised in golf by the recovery of balance, the rotation, and the release of energy towards the target is within each of us. It is a simple, innate action, within reach of us all, like a ricochet or a throw.

The quest for inspired golf is none other than the quest for the self. This was the third great lesson that Édouard shared with me.

He might have been quoting Herrigel, *"He aims and is the target. He shoots and at the same time, is hit"*[57].

In doing so, he revealed the secret of inspired golf to me, he gave me the recipe of the

---

[57]In: Eugen Herrigel: *Zen in the Art of Archery*, op.cit.

magic elixir, the philtre of philtres, the method of all methods, which is no longer a method because it constitutes and surpasses them at one and the same time.

He once told me that to arrive at the essence of golf you must reverse the order of things. Start with what you are aiming at. The target. And with what you are feeling. The sensation linked to the *image* of that target in the distance.

The *image* that takes us to the heart of the reality. Claudel defined the poet as a "teacher of images"[58]. As though one must order images and teach them to teach us. "The educational image"[59].

It is the target that determines the swing. Its routine, its characteristics, its magnitude, its speed. Expressly so that the ball can reach it.

Not the reverse.

And it is the sensation that moves the swing, inspires it and at the same time, constitutes it. Feelings, sensations, and intuition. Not technique.

Fundamentally, therefore, the *swing* is a response to a target. An innate response. A reaction. Which means two things.

---

[58] In : Philippe Barthelet : *Conversations with Gustave Thibon*. Éditions Desclée de Brouwer, Paris, 2016.
[59] ibid.

On the one hand, the swing should never become a goal in itself. An action. It is only a means. A means to reach the target.

On the other hand, the swing must not be merely the expression of opinionated, obstinate, rational, controlled, and conscious practice. Each swing is a deep inhalation, unique, an inspiration that belongs only to he or she who experiences it at a given moment.

Nothing is therefore further from the quest for inspired golf than the construction of a mechanical swing intended to project a ball towards a target in a conscious manner.

On the contrary. An authentic swing contains within it, the All. All the facets of a human being: physical, aethereal, astral, and causal. Mental, divine, and spiritual.

And Édouard would add: if the apprentice golfer positions himself, at best, in relation to the target, the inspired golfer does the opposite. It is the target that positions him.

The greatest players in the history of the game go even further. They have that extraordinary capacity, almost magic, perfectly connected to the intelligible and palpable world, to form one with the ball, the club, and the target.

Even better, they themselves become the target. In the space of an instant, the golfer and the target are no longer two opposing entities, but one and the same reality.

'One shot, one life'[60], as the zen archers liked to say.

The inspired golfer is no longer conscious of himself as a person occupied in aiming at a target. Stripped of all ego and all parasitic thoughts, he is in a state of non-consciousness that allows him to attain the ultimate reality, the essence of things.

A state of non-consciousness that is still consciousness. Since albeit negatively, it is still in relation to this that we determine ourselves, precisely to surpass and transcend it. Non-consciousness or transcended consciousness, which is next to supra-consciousness and also to the unconscious.

Indeed, in inspired golf, the two worlds have merged. The spiritual dimension has 'sublimated' the material dimension. Operating an exquisite alchemy, it has transformed, magnified, and illuminated it for ever.

The inspired golfer is not only reasonable and rational. He is also intuitive and instinctive. He is now able to have an overall vision of the infinitely small and the infinitely large, of the evident and the non-evident.

---

[60]In : Eugen Herrigel: *Zen in the Art of Archery*, op.cit.

Reconciling opposites, benefitting from the ingenious alliance of apparently opposing dimensions, sensing the unity that lies beyond the duality, he creates and accedes at the same time to a new golfing reality.

His golf can attain completeness. It is no longer simply a pastime devoid of meaning, a sporting discipline to be mastered after the repetition of physical exercises and the application of key techniques. It is a spiritual discipline, which thanks to the mind, sensation and intuition allows the player to achieve total self-fulfilment. Total *self*-fulfilment.

This pedagogy, which is also a philosophy therefore disturbs the order of things. Indeed, it paves the way for change.

This pedagogy is a real 'revolution'. Not in the clichéd sense of the word. It is a 'return to the self'. As a reiteration of what has been.

And a forecast of what will be.

XIII.

THE REVELATION

In the Arthurian legends, the revelation is an integral part of the quest. It never marks the end. Indeed, it obeys very precise rules. It is always unexpected and unhoped for. It often takes the form of a dream, a vision or an apparition. It can also be the work of a providential person, an old hermit or a maiden. The revelation often occurs on the day of Pentecost, which celebrates the descent of the grace of the Holy Spirit upon the Apostles. It was then that the Grail appeared for the first time.

The revelations made to the knights are always intended to put them back on the right path when they have gone astray or are prey to terrible doubts.

On a day of great confusion, I asked Édouard what, for him, 'inspired golf' really meant.

I will never forget that magic moment. It happened in an enchanting spot, in between the towns of Randazzo, Linguaglossa and Castiglione di Sicilia, not far from Taormina.

Situated at a height of 650 meters on the northern slope of the volcano, the *Picciolo Golf Club,* with its natural amphitheatre deep within the Etna regional park was, without a doubt, the most beautiful setting I could ever wish for in which to complete my training.

The black lava stones were a reminder of the 1916 eruption and the destructive force of nature. But the luxuriance of the vegetation and wealth of plants, nut trees, forsythia, and especially heather, were also a reminder of its regenerative power.

Everywhere, the volcano was present, revealing its contrasts. Both comforting and benevolent – for the inhabitants of eastern Sicily, Etna is feminine, a protective mother – but also imposing and threatening.

Disarming in their simplicity and clarity, Édouard's words enlightened me.

Inspired golf is 'consciousness' he began by informing me. Consciousness of what is manifested, that is to say, Man and the environment.

Consciousness of what is unmanifested – or not manifested –, that is, sensation and intuition.

Inspired golf is, in its very essence, an interior journey. Intimate. Immense. Intimate immensity. That is its goal, the one that Gaston Bachelard in *The Poetics of Space* evokes when he tells us that *"Immensity is within us […] Immensity is the movement of immobile Man"*[61].

Inspired golf also involves 'mastery', he continued. Mastery of the self, which is above all a forgetting of the self.

Success implies showing unswerving discernment in a world obsessed with performance and success coupled with great humility without which there can be no realisation.

Mastery of the five elements too, which enables mastery of the course. The course, that complex, uncertain equation that requires the player to cope with a string of inconstant and ever-changing variables.

Listening to Édouard, after so many years of following the wrong track and of suffering, I was speechless. Stunned.

I understood that my intellect had been my worst enemy all these years, whilst my brain, on the other hand, was my greatest ally. Moreover,

---

[61] In : Gaston Bachelard, *La Poétique de l'Espace (The Poetics of Space)*, Presses Universitaires de France, Paris, 1958.

the latter had never betrayed me, I had to admit.

Since early childhood it had been constantly preventing me from falling or tripping up. It had been constantly protecting me, through my reflexes, from all the dangers that threatened me. It was constantly on the watch, reducing the risks I was exposed to and finding the most appropriate ways of thwarting them.

By the simple fact of its existence, it was therefore impossible that when I came to execute my swing, my brain would unbalance me or create useless tension or produce a forced, physically difficult, even painful movement. All of which happened, nevertheless. Self-preservation was its very essence. Its ultimate program. I understood that this was because I had not given it the 'right' instructions, the 'right' tasks to do. I had to abandon static positions and feel a dynamic sensation.

The scales dropped from my eyes. It was high time I became a spectator of my golf, and not the actor.

The meaning of 'non-action' or *wuwei*, or more precisely, 'acting without acting' or *wei-wu-wei*, ideas that are central to Taoism, now became clear. I must learn to follow the natural flow of things, without disturbing or attempting to artificially modify them.

This did not mean adopting an attitude of inaction or passivity, but rather the spontaneous attitude, through which the action was performed by enchantment without the assistance of the will[62].

This implied two things.

On the one hand, accepting to accompany 'only' the *momentum*[63], without conscious manipulation thereby enabling me to deliver my action and my energy, without effort, towards my image.

On the other hand, to feel an ample, tensionless backswing, with no resistance whatsoever, with maximum fluidity, in perfect relation to where I wanted my ball to begin its flight, to the right, left, or above an intermediary focal point.

Inspired golf was of a disconcerting simplicity. An intermediate focal point. A target. A flight plan. And the corresponding sensation to carry it out, perfectly relaxed.

I had spent all those years trying to reproduce, even imperfectly, the swing of the cham-

---

[62] See the work of Professor Edward Slingerland who drew a parallel between the ancient Chinese philosophy and the cognitive neurosciences concerning the way *wuwei* works: *Trying Not to Try, Ancient China, Modern Science and the Power of Spontaneity*, Crown (Random House), New York, 2014.

[63] *Momentum* is the combination of the 'right' swing and the 'right' speed.

pions I admired. A movement reputed to be perfect. Vertical, ample, fast.

I understood at last the extent to which I had been mistaken. The perfect movement was not a mathematical, geometrical, analytical movement. The perfect movement was that which corresponded to an image: my target, whatever it was and wherever it was.

This was the secret of inspired golf.

And that too of Ben Hogan, without a doubt the most elegant golfer of all time, who confided, a touch enigmatically, *"my secret is easy to find if I tell you where to look"*.

The truth cannot be possessed. It subjugates. And I had at last opened my eyes. I now knew where to look.

XIV.

CONSCIOUSNESS OF MAN

itruvian Man, the inspiration for the logo of *Wisdom in golf*, is doubtless one of the best-known drawings in the world. Drawn in 1492 by Leonardo da Vinci, it highlights the perfect proportions of the human body according to the Roman architect-engineer, *Vitruvius*[64]. The drawing shows an ideal that makes proportion and arithmetic a condition of the beauty of the human body[65]. But not only.

---

[64]In : Vitruvius : *De Architectura*, Book III, written around -15 BC.
[65]In : Laetitia Marcucci : *'L'homme vitruvien' et les enjeux de la représentation du corps dans les arts à la Renaissance ('Vitruvian Man' and Issues of the Representation of the Human Body in the Arts during the Renaissance)*, Nouvelle revue d'esthétique, n°17, January 2016, p. 105-112, PUF, Paris.

The four sides of the square symbolise the finite nature of matter and the world of reason. The circle represents the infinite nature of the universe and the world of the unintelligible. Movement, suggested by the superposition of the two bodies, allows Vitruvian man to be at the centre of both the square and the circle, allowing him at one and the same time to pass from one to the other and to remain in one and the other.

Vitruvian Man therefore solves the squaring of the circle in an ingenious manner. In doing so, he symbolises Renaissance Man, New Man capable of being reborn thanks to the perfect synthesis that he creates between heaven and earth. Universal Man also, who transcends the material world thanks to the spiritual, the darkness thanks to light, escaping by the same token from his finite nature.

Although Shawn and Édouard do not go as far as Vitruvius in the mathematization of the representation of the human body, on the other hand, they never cease repeating that golf should be fully based on respect for both body and mind.

Respect for the body. A perfect knowledge of the human anatomy is at the heart of this apprenticeship.

How is the body formed? Which movements give width and produce energy? Where are the constraints likely to cause injuries and pain? How does the body react to the practice of golf?

Édouard never stopped asking me questions on human anatomy and explaining it to me. All his pupils were introduced to *Skully*, his faithful skeleton.

The need to be constantly listening to one's body. Édouard was insistent: the body can prove to be a teacher as wonderful as it is unexpected. He is constantly encouraging the pupil to adapt his play and practice to his physical characteristics, morphology, and muscles.

Like Moe Norman, now and for ever Édouard's other spiritual father, who after long practice sessions, on return to the changing room after 'hitting' hundreds of balls, observed with scientific rigour how his body had reacted in order to improve his swing. The muscles that ached were those that had been used the most. He deducted that he must make them even more supple to gain greater elasticity and muscle tone. Moe confided once that he soaked his hands in blood and his arms in boiling water. Every part of his body was carefully reviewed up to and including his eyes to determine which of them was the more tired and had played a more active role.

Édouard pointed out to me one day that the players who left their mark on the history of golf in the first half of the twentieth century, from Walter Hagen to Bobby Jones, and including Ben Hogan, all had fluid swings, with no resistance, and with maximum width and rotation, swings that totally respected the human body.

Their swings were poetry in motion. They embodied the very essence of 'abandon of control'. Studies also showed that they suffered far fewer injuries than contemporary players even though they were using often rudimentary equipment without the benefit of modern technology. They were doubtless less powerful than today's players but the grace they displayed has never been equalled.

Respect for the brain.

I was surprised to discover the extent to which Édouard had studied the question. The way the brain works is still not fully understood despite great advances in the neurosciences. Its main functions have nonetheless been clearly identified. The main function of the brain is to control the actions of the organism based on the sensorial information that reaches it. The capture of external *stimuli* allows it to be permanently creating responses to the environment.

Moreover, Édouard never ceased telling me that the brain was 'allergic' to repetition. It can only reproduce and imitate imperfectly. Its main aptitude consists in learning, innovating, and continually adapting.

The aim of the quest for inspired golf could not therefore be the mastery of 'repetition'. It necessarily had to favour 'inventiveness'.

And Édouard warned me: the apprentice golfer should ensure he does not become a *driving range* player. Accustomed to using the driving ranges almost exclusively, he tirelessly repeats the same strokes with the same clubs and the same targets. Nothing could be further from the true spirit of golf. And from the fairways.

Driving range, an artificial world cut off from reality, source of all illusions and all dangers. Like Lancelot, in the Lost Forest, prisoner of the *Magic Carol* that suspends time, drawn into a deafening farandole that he cannot or will not leave, to the great despair of his valet.

The main difficulty of golf, which is also its main point of interest, lies precisely in the variety of strokes it requires the golfer to master: targets, lies, height of the grass, uneven terrain, balance, consistency of the ground, obstacles, and permanently changing weather conditions.

All this requires creativity, daring and sometimes even imagination. The inspired golfer is also an artist; the art, sublime and subtle that through pleasure, admits the world of the senses into the field of consciousness.

XV.

CONSCIOUSNESS OF PLANET EARTH

Cartography was developed and flourished during the Middle Ages. Many false ideas surrounding it are still circulating today, such as the claim that the scholars of the time thought that the Earth was flat. Fra Mauro's map of the world, drawn in 1450, is a key work in western cartography[66].

Travellers, merchants, and pilgrims were constantly expanding the horizons. The contours of the earth were becoming clearer, even though, in the Christian world, maps were

---

[66]In : Christiane de Craecker-Dussart, *La cartographie médiévale : d'importantes mises au point (Medieval Cartography : Important Developments)*, Le Moyen Âge (The Middle Ages), 2010/1 (Volume CXVI), p.165-175, Édition De Boeck Supérieur, Louvain-La-Neuve.

drawn in accordance with religious beliefs and not always for practical purposes[67].

The study of physics was also advancing fast. Jean Buridan, Nicole Oresme, and Thomas Bradwardine showed great innovation and force of character in their accounts of the finite nature of the cosmos, the speed of projectiles and the fall of bodies[68].

Shawn and Édouard issued constant reminders of this: golfers are above all, "Humans on Planet Earth".

Moreover, inspired golf also draws on total respect for the environment and an understanding of the laws governing the universe and our planet.

More than technique, it is the laws of physics, most importantly those governing gravity and centrifugal force that play a fundamental role in learning inspired golf.

Gravity, by exalting the weight of the arm-club unit, enables it to produce the natural arc of a swing without any manipulation at all. To which Édouard would always add the reminder that all human beings are experts in gravity. Gravity began with the emergence of the Earth

---

[67] ibid.
[68] In : Edward Grant : *La physique au Moyen Âge : VIe -XVe siècles (The physics of the Middle Ages: 6th-15th centuries)*, PUF, Paris, 1995.

more than four billion years ago. Playing golf without using this marvellous force, intangible physics, is a nonsense. Apostasy. Heterodoxy.

Feeling gravity was, however, not so simple. I understood that being 'subject' to it was one thing, being aware of it and using it voluntarily was another. I experienced very great difficulties because it meant starting with a clean slate, banishing all parasitic thoughts. Unlearning, again and again. Unlearning control of the various sequences of the swing.

To help me feel gravity, Édouard began by explaining that each of my arms weighed around nine per cent of my total body weight. If we add to this the weight of the golf club, the arm-club unit represents a significant load. Learning to use this heaviness, similar to the weight of an axe or a mace, was primordial in order to swing effortlessly through the ball, the grass and the ground in the direction of the target.

Édouard's insistence paid off. I finally succeeded in becoming aware of this weight and using it wisely. The rhythm of my swing became naturally slower. My body learnt to cope with this new force, liberating a hitherto unknown power. I could feel the *momentum*, the abandon of control. Effortlessness became a reality. As Édouard said, when you swing a golf club, there are always two of you: yourself and gravity.

Another force completed the effects of gravity. Centrifugal force. For Shawn and Édouard, it was the second vital element of all inspired golf.

The term is inappropriate because strictly speaking, centrifugal force is not a force. Physics only recognises centripetal force, the force that pulls back to the centre. It would be more accurate to call it a centrifugal effect.

Édouard explained to me that the centrifugal effect enabled the creation of speed, without tension, a role that could not be accomplished by the arms alone. It was the centrifugal effect, on the other hand, that set the arms in motion. Moreover, it was at the origin of one of the most sought-after sensations in golf: that of the arms literally 'pulled' 'drawn' or 'sucked' towards the target. Provided one has the necessary width.

In addition to gravity and the centrifugal force, Édouard also taught me little by little to deal with all the elements of Planet Earth. They were precious allies in the quest for inspired golf.

The ground is an extraordinary generator of power. Thanks to the downswing weight shift. Head in the clouds, for sure. But feet on the ground, firmly, inexorably, planted.

Grass is a basic component to inspired golf. Édouard never stopped repeating that a golf club is not a lever or compressor of a little white ball. A golf club serves to cut the grass. High or not so high, thick, or less thick. Green or not so green. It is the best way to feel the release of energy towards the target. The *grass whip*[69] is one of Shawn's favourite tools.

Coastlines, borders, and promontories are marvellous natural targets. Édouard also contributed to expanding my horizons.

He told me one day that Moe Norman, without a doubt the most accurate golfer of all time, had a very special way of visualising his strokes: he would choose the height of his shot and in relation to the height, the elements of the landscape. The trees, their tops, the clouds, and the horizon were just so many colours on the palette of this genius of a painter.

He was an inspired painter who could paint anything with his incredible made-to-measure brushes, on any course in the world. Golf courses: his sublime canvasses that have left imperishable masterpieces, the expression of a unique poetry of natural spaces.

For the inspired golfer, poetry is *"a cartography that allows one to gaze in the direction of*

---

[69]Tool used to cut grass.

the Beyond."⁷⁰ Landscapes become a sensorial space, a fictional geography, an inner space. *"A topography of the soul, that is what you are"*, wrote Marina Tsvetaïeva to Rainer Maria Rilke in a letter she wrote to him on 12 May 1926⁷¹.

---

⁷⁰In : Jean-Michel Maulpoix, *Les 100 mots de la poésie (The 100 Words of Poetry)*, Que sais-je, PUF, Paris, March 2018.
⁷¹ibid.

XVI.

NON NOBIS

Non nobis, domine, non nobis, sed nomini tuo da gloriam[72]. The motto of the Knights Templar, the Order of the 'The poor fellow-soldiers of Christ and of the Temple of Solomon' that appeared in the 12th century A.D under the impetus of Bernard de Clairvaux, is well-known. The monk-soldiers intended this to underline the humility that should be *de rigueur* in the Order. To be humble is to be good 'hummus'[73]

---

[72]*"Not unto us, O Lord, not unto us; but to your name be the glory."*
[73]In : *Historique, légende, et symbolisme de la Table Ronde, mythe fondateur de la Chevalerie Spirituelle chrétienne (History, Legend and Symbolism of the Round Table, Founding Myth of Christian Spiritual Knighthood).* Lecture given by Bernard Reydellet, presented by the

to plant and grow the spiritual seeds that are in all human beings.

Édouard was constantly emphasising that inspired golf is above all a state of mind. Everything is within us. Everything is around us. We therefore need to restore harmony with ourselves and with nature.

The teacher is only there for a time to correct some of the disharmony that exists between the human body and brain and the environment in which we live. He is simply there to enlighten, to act as a mirror. His ultimate purpose is to help the pupil become aware of his strengths and aware of the forces that surround him.

Édouard gradually made me understand that inspired golf was nothing other than Chinese medicine. Above all, it was preventive medicine. Frequent consultation of the practitioner was an admission of failure.

He explained to me one day that pupils should spend only a limited amount of time with him. In the beginning, I was astonished, and it was only much later that I understood what he meant.

Pathologies are simply the expression of a lack of balance or harmony with oneself and

---

Association of the *Collège Templier*, in collaboration with the Cadences bookshop – Lyon.
http://www.le-college-templier.com/Actualité.

with nature, and one must simply find and heal the causes to ensure a return to a normal state. This pre-supposes that human beings are intrinsically in good health and in harmony with the environment in which they live. The swing that is naturally and carefully planted in each of us therefore simply needs to be discovered and fully expressed, not constantly repaired, corrected, healed, and manipulated.

This medicine is consequently based on the rigorous observation of nature and human beings, considered as a dynamic unit. It therefore possesses a highly developed diagnostic system based on three phases: interrogation, observation and listening.

Édouard was constantly insisting on the fact that one must always be willing to learn from one's mistakes. He would also add, surprisingly, that to progress, feedback[74] from the pupil was vital, doubtless more so than the teacher's view.

What is important above all, is to establish an accurate diagnosis of the situation, determining after each shot if one remained concentrated on the target during the whole movement, to judge the balance achieved, to assess the level of effort generated by our body and to analyse the speed produced.

---

[74] Observation of the stroke played.

Between master and pupil, a complex relationship is established that is deep and virtuous. The one is constantly learning from the other.

Teacher and pupil. Arthur and his knights. Arthur, model of wisdom and courtesy, giving infallible, benevolent support to his knights, encouraging them to prove their courage and always give full measure of their physical and moral valour. The knights, obliged to respond to this infallible and benevolent support through continuous exploits that in return, enhance the glory of the king and his court.

This reciprocal learning between master and pupil involves total humility on the part of one and the other. The abandonment of the *ego*. Of the 'I'.

The *non nobis*. Renouncing. Detachment. The forgetting of the 'self' that leads to the gift of the 'self'. And above all, to zen. The intuition that the teacher is pupil and the pupil, teacher.

"My pupils are my teachers"[75].

---

[75]*Leitmotiv* in Shawn and Édouard's *Wisdom in Golf* pedagogy.

PART TWO

INSPIRATION (MASTERY)

"We must become like children again through long years of training in the art of forgetting the self".

DAISETZ T. SUZUKI

XVII.

SALISBURY

he defeat at Salisbury hastened the mysterious end of King Arthur and put an end to the adventurous times. *Salisbury*, the pre-destined plain often mentioned by Merlin in his prophesies and which was to leave the Kingdom of Logres an orphan. *Salisbury*, scene of King Arthur's last battle and his defeat by Mordred's army, which was twice as big and made up, moreover, of rebel barons, Saxons on whom the King had inflicted so many humiliations and defeats in the past.

My first golf course with Édouard was also a real disaster. A bitter, cruel experience. A scalding defeat of the sort that can wound the soul and not only the body and mind.

It was situated in the Roman countryside not far from the Coliseum, another place steeped in history and above all, in dust, tears, and blood.

Located in a magical setting, the *Archi di Claudio Golf Club* is a little jewel set against the backdrop of the sumptuous vestiges of the eighth Roman aqueduct begun under the Emperor Caligula in the year 38 and completed under the reign of the Emperor Claude in August 52, almost 800 years after Rome was founded.

Without a doubt, I had never, in all my life, been so keen to play well. It was a question, not of winning some trophy or prestigious prize, but of showing my master that I had understood all the subtleties and profundity of his message. That I was at one with his pedagogy and philosophy. That I was worthy of being his disciple.

Never, in all my life, did I play so badly.

That day, I understood that the course was a world apart, that nothing could replace it. Neither the driving range nor training sessions, however well suited they might be.

I also understood that Édouard had more than once warned me of this. To be in a "real life game situation", to "transport" onto the course all the work invested in the training sessions was one of the greatest difficulties facing all apprentice golfers.

He was constantly preparing me for this painful, but salutary experience. He knew it. It was inevitable. Another unavoidable stage in the apprenticeship of inspired golf. I had remained deaf to his warnings.

Being aware of illusions and enchantments of all kinds, learning to use one's sensations wisely, knowing how to trust one's intuition rather than following one's instinct: initiation to the course must necessarily complement the initiatory journey.

XVIII.

ENCHANTMENT

Like the Knights of the Round Table in the Forest of Broceliande with Merlin, Melusine, and Viviane, the apprentice golfer must learn that things are not always what they seem. Like the spells and enchantments used by the fairies and magicians to divert the knights from their quest, in golf, appearances are often deceptive, artificial, and fallacious and can have disastrous consequences.

Indeed, the apprentice golfer must overcome many trials in the pursuit of his quest. Trials that although they no longer involve some terrifying enemy, man, beast or demon, are nonetheless formidable.

These ordeals relate to visual perceptions. The apprentice golfer must correct his vision. He must learn to no longer see either the ball or the obstacles.

For a long time, the ball was my worst enemy. My greatest illusion. Indeed, one rule brooked no exception in my game: I never 'missed' my practice swings. When I asked Édouard about this one day he gave me an explanation that was as disconcerting as it was obvious: it was because there was no ball. And, he insisted, trying to lift or compress a little white ball and send it with all one's might as far as possible is doubtless the biggest mistake the apprentice golfer can make. It is a trap. A trick.

Moreover, Édouard identified two main categories of swing. On the one hand, swings towards a ball, which are often the preserve of beginners and which always produce the same patterns: sway[76], reverse pivot, restrained backswing, an over the top action, slice, top, fat shot, pull[77], push[78], hook, deep divot[79], no divot

---

[76]Sideways movement of part of the body preventing it from pivoting on a stable axis.
[77]Trajectory of a ball that flies too far to the left of the target line for a right-handed player, too far to the right for a left-handed player.
[78]Trajectory of a ball that flies too far to the right of the target line for a right-handed player, too far to the left for a left-handed player.
[79]Strip of grass gouged out by the club as it passes under the ball and that must be put back in place.

at all, half top, weak grip, chicken wing[80], loss of balance, absence of finish.

On the other hand, swings towards a target, which are those of the best players and which all display the same characteristics: a backswing in relation to the target, lag, tilt[81], a pause at the top of the backswing, a return of the club from the inside, a powerful downswing weight shift, a balanced centre of gravity, a ball-grass-ground contact, width, speed, compression, rhythm, abandon of control, extension, release, finish.

To show a lack of interest in the ball, to detach oneself from it, to not acknowledge it, is the most difficult thing to do in golf. The fact is that since it is immobile, it monopolises the attention of the brain and body that seek to make it move. At any price.

Édouard's verdict was final. The result of this was the establishment of a setup[82] based entirely on physical force and a controlled, conscious action. It was the perfect response of the body and brain to the erroneous command that had been transmitted to them: lift or compress a

---

[80] When the body stops turning opposite the ball – the default target – during impact, with the arms crashing against the rib cage. The folded arms take on a shape reminiscent of a chicken wing.
[81] Angle of the axis of the spine needed to hit the ball in profile, for example, a ricochet.
[82] Initial organisation.

motionless ball. Furthermore, Édouard explained that on the contrary, one should give the body and brain the possibility of reacting to an appropriate neurological command. Indeed, the brain must learn to respond to dynamic external commands and the body to accomplish new tasks.

Cutting the grass with a grass whip. Driving nails into door frames with a hammer. Whittling bamboo with a sword. Splitting wood with an axe. All Édouard's pupils repeated these exercises an infinite number of times, rather like young Daniel San in *Karate Kid*, required by Master Miyagi to paint fences, wash cars and catch flies with chopsticks to learn the art of combat and pierce the secrets of karate[83].

The apprentice golfer should not be afraid to use unusual means nor to take a detour to achieve his objective. Detours, annoying though they may be, are always preferable to the absence of a path.

Obstacles are omnipresent on the golf course. However, Édouard made a remark one day that gave me food for thought for a long while: for the best players in the world, there is no obstacle. They never see the water nor the woods nor the out-of-bounds. Professional players only see the place where they want their

---

[83] In : John G. Avildsen, *Karate Kid*, film made in 1984.

ball to land. Better still, for them, the obstacles become favoured targets. The bunkers, for example, allow them to avoid a more dangerous rough, or a more awkward configuration.

Édouard therefore encouraged me to replace what frightened me on the course by what I wanted to do. He encouraged me to display positive visualisation.

He explained to me that the latter can show itself in two ways, the first being the ideal solution.

One can, for example, learn to forget the obstacles and focus exclusively on the target, the landing place or point where the ball falls. Positive visualisation is thus directed at the materialisation of an objective to be reached. The player's concentration is exclusively turned towards the 'correct' trajectory and height of the ball, and on the corresponding image and sensation.

Or, on the contrary, one can observe with the greatest attention the configuration of the hole and therefore the obstacles and so devise an appropriate strategy. *"Where can I 'miss' my shot without too much damage"*? *"Where, above all, should I not send my ball"*? Positive visualisation is used here to take the 'right' decisions and gain more confidence.

The inspired golfer is inhabited by an unshakeable faith. He knows that otherwise his quest may become a labyrinth from which there is no escape. Fatal.

XIX.

SENSATION

Grip, pressure of the hands, posture, alignment, rotation, transfer of weight, movement of the arms; entire books have been devoted to each of these key elements in the golf *swing*. All, however, tackle the technical aspects to the exclusion of all else. Strangely, none mention the sensations that must necessarily be linked to these.

At first, Édouard's observation left me puzzled but I soon had to face the fact that he was correct.

This was a challenge. Deprived of sensations, the teaching of golf was necessarily lacking in something; amputated, imperfect, like a white rose with no perfume. This could only leave the apprentice golfer frustrated. Frustrated, because senseless. Deprived of the senses.

Édouard explained to me that the different sequences of the swing could be "felt" but that they were never completely "understood".

It was telling, he continued, that when professional players were asked what they concentrated on when about to play a shot, rare were those who mentioned a key technique, a particular sequence of the swing, or an exercise they were in the habit of practising in training. They almost always mentioned, on the other hand, the target they were visualising, their current state of mind, or the sensations they were experiencing. And, he concluded, for the apprentice golfer, it was essential to become familiar with a set of perceptions and emotions that would serve as tonalities in their game. The task was delicate. I learnt this to my cost.

The sensation linked to the "right" pressure of the hands, for example, is difficult to feel. It calls for a heightened sense of touch, extreme sensitiveness. But above all, it is different for everyone and is constantly changing depending on the environment, the force of the wind, temperature, and the shot to be played.

Playing a chip shot[84] downhill fifty metres from the flag in summer on very dry ground does not require the same hand pressure as playing an iron in a very thick rough, a hundred

---

[84] Small shot in the direction of the green.

and forty metres from the flag in winter on slippery or wet ground.

The sensation linked to the "correct" or "dynamic" posture as it is known, is that of being "sucked into" the ground thanks to gravity and the weight of the body perfectly distributed in the centre of the arc of the feet as though the latter were suction cups.

Others spoke of a sensation linked to a cross. A balanced cross in which the two axes were of equal length. At the point where the horizontal line – space – and the vertical line – time – meet, at the intersection of these two lines of equal strength, is born the single, unmoveable, intangible point, the centre of gravity. A real alchemist's crucible, source of balance and strength.

The "correct" alignment can also only be found through the "correct" sensation. Here, it is the target that plays a determining role along with the environment. Together, they send information that "suggests" the trajectory to be adopted, the appropriate height of the ball, the satisfactory speed, the "right" shot, and the appropriate rhythm.

All this serves to create in each player a perception that has more to do with "emotion" than technique. This emotion is linked to an "intention", the intention to play a particular shot in a specific context at a given moment to respond to a precise image; that sketched, outlined, drawn by the target.

The sensation linked to rotation is often described by Édouard as that of the Medieval catapult. The trebuchet. The mangonel.

Armed with a solid posture, the apprentice golfer must learn to use his posterior as a counterweight. This counterweight is an incredible generator of energy, power, and speed. It quite literally enables the arms and the projectile – the club and not the ball – to be "catapulted" towards the target.

Finding the "correct" sensation in relation to the movement of the arms is not easy either. Attention is too often focused on the backswing. Identifying the "correct" backswing, the "correct" placement of the arms, the "correct" angles and the "correct" plan often wrongly monopolises the concentration and work of the apprentice golfer.

Obsessed by technique, back to the target, turned towards the teacher and not towards the objective, the learner is often in the preponderance of the "I" that allows control, and in that of power that encourages physical strength, rather like the priests, who in the Middle Ages, began celebrating Mass with their backs to the altar, turned towards the congregation and no longer towards God, becoming "power" and ceasing to be "authority". It was a time when these ideas were confused, with the partisans of the Pope desiring all the powers and those of the Emperor accepting no authority.

This is regrettable. Édouard is categorical: letting the arms and the club "react" naturally rather than responding to "manipulation" teaches the apprentice golfer three fundamental things: not to precipitate his action, to remain "passive" on the return, and to remain connected to the target.

Patience: he waits. Wisdom: he lets go. Discernment: he is sure of his prediction.

The apprentice golfer penetrates little by little into the heart of inspired golf.

XX.

INTUITION

In the 13th century, for the first time, Cardinal Matteo d'Aquasparta, a Franciscan philosopher and theologian extended the theological concept of intuition, traditionally used to explain the beatific vision, the view that the chosen have of God in Heaven, to the question of self-knowledge[85]. Indeed, he details the boundaries of the concept of intuition. Intuition is an interior vision that contributes to the immediate and direct knowledge of one's self.

---

[85]In : Ana Irimescu : *De l'intuition au Moyen Âge à la connaissance intuitive chez Jean Duns Scot*, *(From Intuition in the Middle Ages to Intuitive Knowledge in Jean Duns Scot)* doctoral thesis in philosophy, under the direction of Olivier Boulnois, defended on 12 December 2015 in Paris (*École Pratique des Hautes Études*).

In the stories of the Round Table, intuition often decides the fate of the knights. Presentiment or inspiration, of sacred or profane origin, coming from the depths of their being or with the benevolent help of an unknown voice, intuition is either a warning or it enlightens them in the quest for the Grail.

For a long time, Perceval is ignorant of his lineage and name. Then one day, he has an intuition. The revelation of his name coincides with the discovery of who he really is[86]. La Pucelle suspects that Lancelot is in love with Guinevere[87]. Gawain guesses that the black knight has put on Galehaut's armour[88]. Arthur's presentiments herald his imminent death in his fight against Mordred. Merlin sees Viviane's intention to imprison him for ever in the invisible prison.

---

[86] In : Barbara N. Sargent-Baur, *La destre et la senestre* : Étude sur le Conte du Graal de Chrétien de Troyes (*Dexter and Sinister*: Study on the Story of the Grail by Chrétien de Troyes), Faux Titre, n°185, Éditions Rodopi B. V., Amsterdam - New York, 2000.

[87] In : Philippe Ménard : Le rire et le sourire dans le roman courtois en France au Moyen Âge (1150-1250), (*The Laugh and the Smile in Medieval French Courtly Romances*), Publications romanes et françaises, Librairie Droz, Geneva, 1969.

[88] ibid.

Like the characters in the Arthurian legends, how can the apprentice golfer learn to use his intuition wisely?

Édouard told me one day that more than two hundred and thirty-two muscles, working together in just a few fractions of a second, were involved in the execution of the golf swing. Analysing the role of each, studying their function in order to use them to best advantage, in a conscious way, was therefore impossible.

Inspired golf only takes on its full meaning in the abandon of control, in the intuitive. Understanding the intuitive, however, and above all to feel it, is no easy task.

Although intuition calls upon forces that have always been in each of us, these primal forces are "innate", unconscious, and unthinking.

Intuition is contrary, by definition, to all that is "acquired", that is, all that is linked to expertise or mastery.

Intuition is the expression of an inner regard. Doubtless that spoken of by the Little Prince when he affirmed that "we only see really well with the heart. That which is essential is invisible to the eyes"[89].

Inspired golf does not, however, set these two orders - visible and invisible - up against

---

[89]In : Antoine de Saint-Exupéry, *Le Petit Prince (The Little Prince)*, Reynal & Hitchcock, New York, 1943.

each other. Quite the contrary. It aims to reconcile them.

Édouard never stopped reminding me that to deny the strategic component of golf is a nonsense. The apprentice golfer must constantly "analyse" the shot he is preparing to play, judge the distance, visualise the trajectory of the ball, take into account the environment and weather, the configuration of the hole, the characteristics of the green, the obstacles, the out-of-bounds, the lies, the height of the rough, the slopes, the state of the ground, the state of the terrain, and his state of mind.

He must be reasonable and rational, constantly observing and learning. In a sense, he must adopt a scientific approach.

Yet golf is an inexact science and therein lies both its beauty and its difficulty. The analytical component will not suffice.

Inspiration, clairvoyance, and flair. The difference between an extraordinary game and an average game is often extremely tenuous and can only be seen in a succession of tiny details, anodyne in appearance.

These little "nothings" that became the "all" in golf. The imperceptible details.

To the scientific approach, must therefore be added a more metaphysical, empirical dimension – understood as sensory experience.

As in a game of chess, the brain is permanently solicited on a golf course. It must continually make choices and arbitrate. Whether to favour a "statistical" or an "intuitive" approach is, for example, a dilemma it faces every second: the choice of club, which stroke to play, and in particular, the trajectory and height of the ball.

Over and over again on the course, Édouard made me play "statistical" shots and "intuitive" shots.

The "statistical" shot is that which relies on technique and game strategy. Rational, it lies at the point where expertise and experience meet. The statistical shot is predictable. It brings the greatest certainty in terms of prediction.

The "intuitive" shot goes against all rational supposition. Despite the player's expertise and experience of the game, it suggests adopting a different approach and playing the shot differently. The "intuitive" shot is moved by an inner sensation, an emotion that seems to indicate which shot would be perfect to play at a given moment, in a particular context. By its very nature, the "intuitive" shot is riskier since it does away with analysis and expertise.

I remember a green bordered by a water hazard to its right. In a sublime setting, situated just a few paces from the summer residence of the Popes in an ancient volcanic crater at the foot of the *Castel Gandolfo* rock. The flag was placed to the right of the green. When the time came for my approach, hundred and thirty metres from the hole, right in the middle of the fairway, I found myself faced with a choice regarding the trajectory of the ball: playing a "statistical" shot or an "intuitive" shot.

Édouard explained to me that the "statistical" shot is based on the supposition that the amateur player has more control over the start of the ball's trajectory than its finish, so the recommended "statistical" shot is always to start the ball towards the spot where there is no danger. Since the flag was placed to the right of the green where the water hazard was also situated, the "statistical" shot would mean opting for a left to right trajectory (fade).

The objective would be to send the ball to the left of the green, the safer part, and then gradually reach the flag on the right-hand side. If the shot were imperfectly executed, the worst-case scenario would be that the ball would not turn at the end of its trajectory. It would remain on the left-hand part of the green, but would not arrive at the water hazard, thereby limiting the damage. If successful, however, the ball would go towards the flag.

Then Édouard explained to me that the "intuitive" shot here consisted of playing a right to left trajectory (draw) that would start with the water in the line of sight, to then turn and land near the flag, to the right of the green. The "intuitive" shot left little room to manoeuvre, however. It had to be perfectly executed on pain of immediate sanction because if the ball did not turn, it would end up in the water.

All golfers have experienced a situation where they have changed club at the last minute, prompted by a sensation that runs counter to the course of action dictated by reason, their analysis of the game, experience, and expertise. A sensation stronger than that ordered by their brain.

What happened?

The player has had a strong *feeling*. A *feeling* that differs from the shot he was preparing to play. And he had the deep-seated conviction, without being able to explain it, that this *feeling* was the right solution for the shot he was about to play. At the last minute, he puts away his sand wedge to run with a 7-iron while he is sixty metres away from the flag. He puts his driver[90] back in his bag and takes a 3-wood on a long, narrow par 5. He takes a 3-iron because he is hitting into the wind on a genuine link[91] in a golf

---

[90]Club usually used at the tee when maximum distance is required.
[91]Course on the coast, generally free of trees.

course running along the sea. He puts away his putter and choses a hybrid to putt[92], from just off the green, in a rough that is thicker than expected.

Intuition is, intrinsically, linked to *perception*. That is its strength but also its weakness. It is its strength because perception invariably exalts the inventiveness and creativity of each person. It is its weakness because it is irreversibly linked to our state of mind – and mood. A parasitic thought, an unwelcome impulse and the intuition of the apprentice golfer can become his worst enemy.

Intuition strongly exalts the duality that is in each of us, the interpenetration of contrary forces, the entanglement of opposites.

Intuition is also a *revelation*. "Direct clarity" wrote Victor Hugo in his *Proses philosophiques*[93].

It reminds us that Man cannot be reduced to his physical dimension. The apprentice golfer must take care not to abandon himself to the fatality of instinct, nor to the sweet intoxication of pride. He must force himself to exalt the divine and spiritual dimensions that lie within him.

---

[92]Action that consists of executing a putt.
[93]In : Victor Hugo : *Proses philosophiques, Philosophie, deuxième partie, l'âme (Philosophical Prose, Philosophy, Second Part, the Soul)*, 1860-1865.

As Victor Hugo points out: *"the extension of intuition, is God"*[94], before concluding, mystically, *"it is because it is superhuman that we must believe in it; it is because it is mysterious that we must listen to it; it is because it seems obscure that it is luminous"*[95].

---

[94]ibid.
[95]ibid.

XXI.

MASTERY OF THE SELF

n the 6th century, whilst King Arthur and the Knights of the Round Table were engaged in their quest for the Holy Grail, performing an incalculable number of exploits and facing momentous challenges, at around the same period in the Orient, Zhiyi, Grand Chinese Master of Tiantai, was disseminating and developing Buddhist teachings and in particular, the Truth of the Middle Way.

All human beings are made up of a physical and a spiritual or insubstantial, dimension, that they must be permanently trying to reconcile through the wisdom and vital energy that bathes the universe and can be seen in all phenomena. Because the Middle Way leads to the attainment of awakening and to liberation from suffering. For the apprentice golfer, it is therefore a precious resource.

Finding the Middle Way is not easy. It is only possible after having experienced the way of extremes.

Édouard liked to remind me that in putting, for example, to find the 'right' swing, it may be useful, during the practice swing, to purposely hit a swing that is too short, followed by a swing that is too long, to finish by feeling the swing that lies in the middle. Similarly, Édouard often recommended striking slightly to the right, then slightly to the left to find the 'right' alignment, the middle alignment.

Édouard offered many more examples. To find the 'right' distance and the sensation that goes with it, during an approach at several dozen metres from the green. Or to determine the 'right' spacing between the body and the ball, that which will allow to deliver an action in relation to the target, without a short-circuit.

For a long time, I was totally intransigent in my game. On the fairways, I could not resign myself to accepting my mistakes or bad luck.

Animated by an inappropriate state of mind, I had difficulty containing my anger and was incapable of controlling my emotions. Boiling inside, losing my temper, irritability: zen remained an abstract, and above all, distant, concept.

I was forgetting that a golf course is, above all, a life course, capable of delivering the best and the worst.

Within the space of four hours, I might experience virtually all possible human sentiments, from wild happiness to unreasonable distress. I veered from one extreme to another. Invincible, blessed by the gods, I felt the ardour and passion of a young adolescent. Cast down, unlucky, I felt like an old man, carrying the weight of a difficult life on his shoulders.

Accepting all these age-related states and all these states of mind and coping with all these emotions was not easy. I had not yet realised that failing with equanimity was an important element of the quest for inspired golf.

Experimenting with extremes is, for any apprentice golfer, a unique, irreplaceable experience. Painful, but beneficial.

Like Siddhartha Gautama, the Buddha, who before achieving enlightenment, nirvana, abandoned himself to two forms of excess: a frantic search for carnal and material pleasures as a prince and extreme austerity, involving every possible privation, which almost cost him his life, as an ascetic.

XXII.

MASTERY OF THE FIVE ELEMENTS

mpedocles, a Greek philosopher born in Agrigento, was the first person in the Occident to describe, almost two thousand, five hundred years ago, the four elements that characterise the manifested world: earth, air, water, and fire.

Later, Plato in *Epinomis* and *Timaeus*, then Aristotle in his treatise, *On the Heavens*, introduced a fifth element, the "fifth essence" - or *quinta essentia*[96]: aether.

In Hindu culture, aether (or *Akasha*) designates space. Traditional Japanese culture, the *Kū*, an integral part of the *Godai*, also describes aether as space or emptiness. We may add to this the idea of *time*. Time and space, the intangible contours of the manifested world.

---

[96]From Medieval Latin.

In his quest for inspired golf, the apprentice golfer must try to acquire mastery of these five elements that are to be found on all the golf courses in the world: aether, understood as control of time and space, fire, air, water, and earth.

But even so, he must have the necessary weapons at his disposal. The armour of justice, shield of faith, and a spiritual defence. The Knights of the Round Table did not set off in search of the Holy Grail without their shining armour. Iron headgear, coat of mail or hauberk, helmet, shin guard, arm bands, shield, harness for the horses, lance, sword – their precious equipment never left these "angels dressed in iron"[97].

To compete against the course on equal terms, the apprentice golfer must also possess suitable weapons. Intermediate focal point, central binocular vision, prediction of contact with the ball, new tasks, new images, Édouard never ceased completing my tool kit in a bid to help me master the five elements, an indispensable condition for mastering the golf course.

---

[97]In : Xavier de Langlais : *Le roman du roi Arthur (The Story of King Arthur)*; Volume III, op.cit.

XXIII.

AETHER

he apprentice golfer is "set" in the universe through the cross formed by space and time. A red and gold cross. The cross of blood and light. The red, which symbolises biological blood is transcended by gold, which symbolises spiritual blood.

Mastery of the aether confers mastery of time and space.

Mastery of time.

Remaining rhythmic in all circumstances, was something Édouard insisted upon because rhythm determines the duration of the swing as well as its intensity. The regularity of the "pulse" guarantees a certain tempo, that is, a certain beat, the speed.

Rhythm also determines movement, which sets the distance. Metrics and rhythm are therefore closely linked. Hence the importance of *momentum*, and the practice swing, two essential components of Shawn and Édouard's pedagogy.

Momentum is above all a sensation, that of the ideal rhythm that corresponds to the image and the setup. The practice swing enables the player to both find and feel the *momentum*.

Like the bardic musicians, the apprentice golfer has a choice of notes. He can express a harmonious game and compose a marvellous melody or on the contrary, recite an abominable cacophony.

However, to do well, talent is not enough. Édouard often emphasised this. One must also prepare well and train harder.

Training allows one to set up a routine and become more confident. Preparation minimises uncertainty and reduces risks.

Before putting, for example, Édouard always ensured that I made a detailed survey of the green. Spotting the micro slopes and break lines, assessing the condition of the grass, its graining and resistance, finding the watering points in order to anticipate the "fluid dynamics" (in particular the drainage) are for him indispensable conditions for success. Walking on the green, going round it examining every aspect is vital for sending the "right" commands to the brain, especially in terms of distance and speed.

Similarly, Édouard always encouraged me to visualise the ball entering the hole. For any apprentice golfer this is a decisive sequence that requires the player to predict the trajectory and speed of the ball during its last forty centimetres.

More than in any other stroke, in putting, sensation wins over technique. The sensation of abandoning control in order to feel the weight of the arm/club unit and to allow it to "work" alone, avoiding all manipulation. Sensation of tact and gentleness in order to find the "right" dosage thanks to the three swings (a too short swing, a too long swing, and a middle-distance swing, the "right" swing) that will allow the putter to "track" gravity in the "right" direction, at an appropriate speed. "Tracking" gravity. Édouard's poetry. His marvellous verses that he recites indefatigably, never tiring of them.

Remaining rhythmic on the long shots is also fundamental, especially when using the driver.

The importance of the practice swing in finding the "right" tempo, the sensation that corresponds to the image, that of the target in the distance, is a *leitmotiv* with Édouard.

Although one must let the driver extend far from oneself through gravity and the centrifugal effect in order to observe the arc of the swing and the path it wants to take, there is another key element in Shawn and Édouard's pedagogy that plays a vital role here: perpetual motion. This allows, in effect, the player to align the appropriate swing and speed with the target.

One day, Édouard told me something that contributed to revolutionising my golf, and especially my putting: perpetual motion carries with it a reality that is all too often misunderstood: in golf, one never aligns parts of the human body with the target. One aligns a *momentum*.

Mastery of space.

Essentially, this involves three things: visualising the trajectory of the ball depending on the chosen game strategy: aggressive or defensive, determining the corresponding shot, fade or draw, and choosing the most appropriate height for the ball.

To achieve this, Édouard suggested I do two hitherto untried things: learn to predict the trajectory of the ball and learn to "miss well".

Predicting the trajectory of the ball depends on several elements: position on the starting area, to the left to open up the right of the *fairway*, to the right to aim the area to the left; the positioning of the ball in the arc of the swing, left for a fade, right for a draw; the openness of the club face, more or less pre-closed; and the alignment which depends on the place where the ball should start its journey or finish it, respectively to the right or left of an intermediate focal point.

The intermediate focal point, which is determined thanks to central binocular vision: two other vital components in the search for inspired golf.

Édouard explained to me one day that the "right" alignment in golf could only be found with the central binocular vision. I looked at him in astonishment. What was this all about?

He explained to me that human beings mainly use two types of vision to perform all the tasks of daily life: central binocular vision and peripheral vision. Only the first gives a true picture of distance and relief, stripped of any optical effects, thereby avoiding the parallax error[98]. Peripheral vision is doubtless indispensable but is used for assessing the general environment through compressed and deformed global impressions of the total visual field it delivers.

---

[98]The parallax is the modification of visual reality resulting from the position of the observer to the side.

Édouard told me that one of the main errors in golf was aligning oneself to the side. Only central binocular vision allows one to identify correctly an intermediate focal point situated between the ball and the target, by placing oneself behind the ball, facing the target.

The intermediate focal point is of capital importance: it allows the player to align himself correctly, increases his comfort zone by moving the target forward, closer to where he is standing at address, and, thanks to peripheral vision, enables him to remain connected to the target from start to finish of the swing.

Learning to "miss well" may seem a disturbing assertion. And the fact is that when Édouard mentioned it for the first time, I was somewhat perplexed.

I was intrigued. He enlightened me, saying that learning to "miss well" is to learn to minimise one's mistakes and therefore reduce the penalties at awkward holes, under difficult conditions and in complicated environments. This calls for a great deal of preparation. It is only possible in fact, if the course has been examined and the game strategy well defined beforehand.

Identifying the holes at which it is possible to take more risks, be more "offensive" and those at which it would be better to be very cautious and favour a more "defensive" attitude, is doubtless of great importance.

But this is not enough. What is important above all, at the start of each hole, is to be aware of the places where it is possible to "miss" a shot.

Indeed, there is "miss" and "miss". Once again, Édouard surprised me.

He explained his thought process: sending the ball into a thick rough or a fairway bunker can doubtless be disadvantageous, but not excessively. It must be accepted. Sending the ball out-of-bounds is, on the other hand, dramatic from the point of view of the score, quite apart from the disasters it can produce on a psychological level. It must be avoided at all cost.

Out of bounds, like the forest.

The forest of Broceliande, the Forest of Morois, and the Forest of Gastée. In Medieval stories the forest always symbolises the disorder of the world. It is a wild place, full of brambles and thorns where the most cruel and deceptive of adventures await the knights. It is a strange place, inhabited by all sorts of mysterious, disturbing beings who are ready to bar the way at any moment.

The forest, like the out-of-bounds.

The apprentice golfer must be careful not to place himself in danger for no good reason.

Mastery of space is vital. The geometric space. The aesthetic space. And above all, the intuitive space.

XXIV.

FIRE

A source of heat and light, fire is, in its very essence, ambivalent.

Synonym of beauty and perfection, in its leap towards the sky, a flame "prefigures that of Man who reaches for the sublime"[99]. Fire is associated with wisdom and emotion, as well as with illumination. The fire of the Holy Spirit illumines humankind. It increases its ardour for God.

Whether it is a destructive or purifying element, fire is also a source of disaster and often associated with Hell. Fire was the greatest scourge threatening the towns and countryside in the Middle Ages. Sentence of death by

---

[99]In : Jean-Pierre Leguay, *Le Feu au Moyen Âge (Fire in the Middle Ages)*, Presses Universitaires de Rennes, Rennes, 2008.

burning at the stake or boiling in a cauldron of water was common practice.

Fire was also a powerful obstacle for the Knights of the Round Table. Lancelot was unable to approach Simeon's burning tomb, he could not quell the boiling fountain, he had to avoid the flaming lance that descended on him like lightening. His love affair with Guinevere barred his way to greater perfection "lust, which is the burning of body and soul"[100] diverted him from his quest.

The apprentice golfer too, must learn to work with fire. The ravages of drought may be, in summer, destructive to some degree and contribute largely to the way in which the game is played.

Scorched earth constitutes a real difficulty. Playing a ball that is resting on dry grass or hard ground without grass is not easy.

Édouard explained to me that this situation was similar to that in which the golfer was sometimes forced to play the ball on a dirt track or asphalt path.

He explained to me that the satisfactory execution of a shot depended on the capacity of

---

[100] In : Alexandre Micha, *Essais sur le cycle du Lancelot-Graal (Essays on the Lancelot-Grail Cycle)*, Publications romanes et françaises, CLXXIX, Librairie Droz S.A., Geneva, 1987.

the player not only to predict the "right" contact with the ball, which was of prime importance here, like all shots played on difficult lies, but also to employ the right setup: lifting one's posture to a greater or lesser degree in relation to the ball.

The required collision here consists in taking less – even no – grass and earth after impact. Hitting a *clean* ball[101], then the earth or twigs or dry grass was often the most satisfactory option.

Adopting an appropriate "dynamic" posture means lifting oneself a little at address in order not to place one's centre of gravity too low. The sole of the club should be at the same level as the base of the ball. Care must be taken, however, not to lift it too much, for example to the level of the equator of the ball, because that would result in hitting a top.

The practice swing is essential for determining the appropriate sensation: feeling the club slide or even ricochet slightly, on the ground.

Édouard explained to me that on an asphalt road, the ball should be hit *clean*. In this last situation, releasing towards the target was vital. Actually, if energy was delivered solely towards the ball, there was a risk of injury, since the club might rebound on the tarmac.

---

[101] Describes ball contact where only the ball is hit, without a divot.

The ravages of drought could also have devastating effects on the greens. These might either resemble waste land rather than an English lawn or, on the other hand, become extremely fast, making all readings and predictions difficult. In both cases, attention should be concentrated on *momentum*, the only thing able to limit the damage.

Édouard recommended always performing the three swings to align the momentum as effectively as possible and to display extreme sensitivity. Feeling the weight of the putter more than usual, delegating even more to gravity and abandoning all control was vital.

Mastering fire. Again, and always. An obsession for Mankind. Outer fire. Inner fire.

But also, poetic fire. As the brilliant and enigmatic aphorism of René Char reminds us: *"The ashes of the cold are in the fire that sings rejection"*[102].

---

[102] In : Tineke Kingma-Eijgendaal et Paul J. Smith, *Lectures de René Char (Readings of René Char)*, études réunies, Éditions Rodopi B. V., Amsterdam - New York, 1990.

XXV.

AIR

The air split by the swords of the knights in combat has always exercised a great fascination over the popular imagination.

Whether or not it is associated with the wind, air is, by definition, immaterial, imperceptible, and impalpable. It took Mankind a long time to understand it since it was assimilated into the world of the divine and the hereafter.

Redolent of the supernatural, the air inspires fear and respect, by turns. Fear, because it could be the source of all danger, bringing about storms and hurricanes. In Medieval literature, the air often embodied "a place of wandering and punishment, for traitorous individuals"[103]. An evil force, it took on hostile forms: the wall of air in the Valley of No Return - or the Aerial Prison - that was to exhaust Merlin's powers.

It also commanded respect since air is also a celestial, divine, beneficial manifestation. The literature of the Middle Ages, such as *Le Roman de la Rose*, also associates it with gentleness, purity, whiteness, transparency, and love. Air carries serenity, calm and voluptuousness.

In golf, mastering the element of air is of crucial importance.

Édouard told me that it is when there is a strong wind, often in extreme playing conditions, that we can measure the difference between the professional and the amateur player. Because in this case, practice is not enough. Experience of the game is vital. Creativity too. Playing with or against the wind is a severe test of a player's capacity to invent, innovate and constantly adapt to the elements.

Several seconds earlier, hitting a low fade with an iron might have been the best option, several seconds later it has become the worst and it is preferable to hit a draw with a wood or a hybrid.

---

[103]In : Jean-Pierre Leguay : *L'Air et le Vent au Moyen Âge*, (*Air and Wind in the Middle Ages*), Presses Universitaires de Rennes, Rennes, 2011.

Édouard put me to the test in every conceivable configuration.

In the face of a strong wind, he explained that remaining in the wind and favouring low balls was often salutary. The latter were, in effect, more likely to guarantee better control, as much in terms of trajectory as in terms of distance.

In the long game, he said, it was preferable to use irons rather than woods or hybrids.

However, he told me that playing medium or high balls should not be excluded. One should simply take care to add one or two extra clubs: since the ball would suffer the effects of the wind to a greater extent, it would be braked proportionally.

To hit a chip shot, he taught me to use an 8 or 9-iron, rather than the sand wedge in order to remain in the wind and make the ball roll as much as possible. He also made me practice playing a chip and run with a 7 or 5-iron, and long putts from just off the green, when the fringe had been well mowed, as on Scottish courses.

With the wind coming from behind, Édouard advised me that remaining low into the wind was not necessarily the best solution.

On the long shots, he encouraged me to play either woods, hybrids, or irons indifferently. I simply had to take care to remove one or two clubs, since the ball would be pushed by the wind.

In the short game, he suggested I favour fairly high wedges[104] that were likely to produce spin[105] and work with the wind to play a shot with less effort.

With a strong lateral wind, mastering ball trajectory became vital.

One should always choose the best game option beforehand: playing with or against the wind. The first option was rarely that chosen by professional players since it gave them less control. Indeed, for long shots as for the short game, Édouard recommended me to play against the wind.

In the case of a strong lateral wind blowing from right to left, with a flag placed to the left on the green, hitting a draw would prove to be a high-risk option because the wind might considerably increase the movement of the ball and therefore significantly modify its final trajectory. Playing a fade against the wind was preferable, which would mean starting the ball in the direction of the flag, to the left of an intermediate focal point aligned towards the middle of the green. Since the final fade curve towards the

---

[104]A very open iron used for approach shots to the green.
[105]Particular movement of the ball.

right would be cancelled by the wind, the ball would finish at the flag.

Conversely, in the case of a strong lateral wind blowing from left to right, with a flag placed to the right of the green this time, playing a draw against the wind would doubtless be the best option. The ball should start in the direction of the flag, to the right of an intermediate focal point aligned towards the middle of the green. Since the final draw curve towards the left would be "cancelled" by the wind, the ball should finish at the flag.

Édouard drew my attention to the fact that playing with or against the wind was, above all, a question of prediction: ball decelerated or accelerated, ball deviated to the right or left.

He concluded by saying that the wind should no longer be considered as an obstacle or negative element. On the contrary, it offered an extraordinary opportunity to improve one's game strategy, mastery of distances and ball trajectories, thereby speeding up progress.

Air is an element that when unleashed can present a daunting challenge for the apprentice golfer, rather like that of the windmills for that Ingenious Gentleman *Don Quixote of La Mancha*.

Be that as it may. Armed with fourteen "swords", or a lance, with a chariot, or the faithful horse *Rocinante*, in the company of a caddie[106], or the inseparable *Sancho Panza*, our two heroes triumph over these hostile forces sent by some ill-intentioned "enchanter".

As Edmond Rostand reminds us:

"Because when we attack them, it often happens [...]
That a whirl of their great arms heavy with sails
Hurls you into the mud!... [De Guiche]
Or into the stars!" [Cyrano] [107]

---

[106]Person accompanying the player and carrying his bag.
[107]In : Edmond Rostand, *Cyrano de Bergerac*, Act II, scene VII, Charpentier & Fasquelle, Paris, 1898.

XXVI.

WATER

ater is everywhere in the Arthurian cycle and the story of the Grail.
Enchanted fountains, maleficent marshes, the so-called "Diane" Lake where Lancelot was brought up, the sea that separates Brittany and Great Britain, the vessel of the fairies coming over the sea to fetch the mortally wounded King Arthur, the lake where Excalibur was thrown, the fights to cross over dangerous bridges such as the Sword Bridge under which deep and dangerous waters flowed, the dreams of knights on river banks, "the marvellous voyages of the celestial knights in search of the Holy Grail"[108], water is

---

[108]In : Micheline de Combarieu du Grès, *L'Eau et l'Aventure dans le cycle du Lancelot-Graal (Water and Adventure in the Lancelot-Grail Cycle)*, p111-147; In :

always mysterious, a bearer of danger or salvation, and magic.

Water is another element with which all apprentice golfers must come to terms.

Although water may be a wonderful ally when the fairways are watered properly, favouring very supple contact with the ball and enabling the club to make a lovely divot after impact, this is far from being always the case. Most often, on the golf course, water is merely a source of difficulties.

It either takes the form of all kinds of obstacle that monopolise, wrongly, the attention of the apprentice golfer: seas, oceans, rivers, lakes, ponds, marshes, rivers, streams and artificial basins or it transforms the fairways into sodden ground. In this case, water is not always welcome. Only a ball in a puddle of water or one that is plugged[109] on the fairway allows the player to make a penalty-free drop[110].

L'eau au Moyen Âge (Water in the Middle Ages), Presses Universitaires de Provence, Aix-en-Provence, 1985.

[109] Said of a ball stuck in a bunker on the fairway, the green or elsewhere. The player may move the ball onto the fairway or the green without incurring a penalty.

[110] Action consisting of picking up the ball when it lands in an unplayable spot, then to let it fall from the hand at knee-height. The drop may incur one penalty point.

.

Édouard explained to me that predicting contact was once again a determining factor in playing a successful shot. Care must be taken not to release the golf club too early since it might provoke a "fat" shot, an action that would block contact with the ball, slow down the club and therefore project the ball just a few metres forward.

Édouard warned me more than once that on sodden ground as on a hard, dry surface, what was important above all was to avoid contact with the ground. Indeed, the player should always place the sole of the club at the base of the ball, at the level of the high part of the grass. Finding the appropriate "dynamic" posture and therefore where to place the centre of gravity was, once again, crucial.

Édouard taught me that the hybrids and fairway woods were, on account of their technical characteristics, precious allies on all sodden courses. The surface area of their soles, wider than that of the irons, enabled them to slide better on wet ground, favouring better contact with the ball.

And he would repeat that practice swings, more than ever, were of capital importance in finding the "right" momentum and the "right" sensation, which were similar to those felt when the ball was lying on very high rough: the sensation, in particular, is that of cutting the top of the grass and not the bottom.

Water in a bunker may also not be casual. It may force the apprentice golfer to play the shot without being able to drop the ball, for example when the water is not a puddle but is simply making the sand much harder.

Édouard explained that I had two options in this situation: either to take less sand and the ball almost clean or to revert to the main task of a shot in the bunker, projecting the sand towards the place on the green where I wanted my ball to land. In this first case, I should bear in mind that the ball would roll further on the green since its trajectory would be lower.

A power that generates and regenerates or which destroys, water has several faces. "The Water of Orpheus", "the Water of Prometheus", "the Water of Hermes"[111]. Mysterious and sanctified, primal and mystical. Water manipulated and instrumentalised, a resource and an atomic component. Water reconsidered and revisited, an object of civilisation and urbanity.

Balancing on the fragile thread that separates the sacred water from the ocean of all dangers, the apprentice golfer is necessarily a skilful tightrope-walker.

---

[111]In : Jean-Philippe Pierron : *Qu'est-ce que l'eau ? (What Is Water ?)* H2O, July 2013.

XXVII.

EARTH

arth has always been an object of conquest. Promised land where milk and honey flow, the Holy Land for Christians, the Pure Land of the Buddha Amitābha, califates of the Arab-Muslim world, Roman provinces, the Carolingian Empire, the Visigothic Kingdom, or foundation of the "Judges of Castile", the earth has always fascinated. It enables Mankind to situate itself in space around powerful, unifying symbols.

From this point of view, the Middle Ages are a pivotal period in history. The Middle Ages invented space. Real territoriality emerged.

Governed by political – kingdoms, provinces, counties, seneschals, seigneuries, fiefdoms – or religious – bishoprics, diocese, parishes – authorities, Medieval territoriality advocated physical continuity and human cohesion centred on common ideals and values.

Nonetheless, the Earth remained a fundamentally ambivalent notion: mountainous summits and subterranean depths, primordial earth, that of fertile silt, black, primal, wild, mother earth, ordered, cultivated and ploughed or land of exile, destructive earth, dead: the Earth presents many faces[112]. Indeed, mastering the element Earth is complicated.

Sand, balls in divots and difficult lies, balls plugged in a thick rough, slopes, the nature of the ground and consistence of the fairways, Édouard warned me: playing conditions are varied and this calls for a great deal of preparation.

Sand is omnipresent on golf courses. Rare are the holes that are not associated with a bunker. Édouard surprised me. He told me that exiting a bunker, whether in the centre of the fairway or right next to a green, did not require shots of any great difficulty. Up until now, this was far from being my opinion. He added that these shots simply needed a special setup and a search for a different sensation from that accompanying shots played on the fairways.

To get out of a bunker placed near a green,

---

[112]See : Gilbert Durand, *Symbolisme de la Terre (Symbolism of the Earth)*, Encyclopædia Universalis France, 2000.

the setup involved lowering the centre of gravity to the level of the sand in order to put the sand in the path of the club. The feet should remain firmly anchored to the ground. What was needed for this shot was to project sand onto the green using the sole of the club and the appropriate momentum, to the place where one wanted the ball to land. The ball should simply be considered as yet another grain of sand. Remaining rhythmic, neither accelerating nor decelerating was essential. Effortlessness took again on its full meaning here.

For shots played from the fairway bunkers, the setup was slightly different. The player must be well anchored to the ground with the insides of the feet slightly open. The sensation was that of being solidly held down on both sides by two walls. The feet should remain flat during the entire swing.

Remaining perfectly centred was essential, as was maintaining the tilt, which involved continuing to lean to the left, head slightly behind the ball to increase the chances of releasing towards the target.

Taking the ball first, clean, was also essential. Édouard explained to me that in this case unlike in the case of bunkers situated near the greens, there was no question of taking sand before the ball. The player was, in fact, placed much too far from the flag. Taking up sand would slow down the ball too much, at a risk of projecting it just a few metres outside the bunker.

The posture should be "dynamic", enabling the player to anticipate the "right" collision and the "right" contact with the ball. Compared to the previous shot, the centre of gravity was somewhat lifted. The sensation was that of "throwing" the club, without forcing, towards the target.

Faced with a ball plugged in a bunker, Édouard informed me that the main error consisted in opening the face of the club more and hitting with all one's might into the sand in the hope of getting the ball off the ground. It was the exact opposite that was needed: closing the face of the club by at least thirty degrees then taking a firm grip again.

The ball should be placed a little to the right within the arc of the swing. Moreover, the momentum should be aligned to the right of the flag where the sand should be sent. He also revealed that the main objective was to create a real trench in the sand upon impact. Only by doing this could one make the ball take off and travel to the green.

He also warned me that since the ball tended to roll a lot, this absolutely had to be taken into account. The "right" collision was sand, then ball.

The ball in a divot is the most characteristic and perfect example of a difficult lie. The principal danger consists in focusing one's attention exclusively on the divot. This inevitably has two negative consequences: from a technical point of view it takes the apprentice golfer out of his comfort zone since his expertise in the matter is limited, and psychologically, it suggests to him that he has had bad luck, which causes tension and anger, which means he cannot play the shot in the best possible state of mind.

Édouard told me that it was above all important to maintain one's focus on the target. Predicting the "right" contact with the ball presupposed placing the sole of the club on the level of the divot, at ground height, in other words, a little lower than usual.

The *release* of energy happened thanks to a firmer pressure from the hand, since the earth that had to be taken up upon impact was more resistant than grass.

Playing a ball that lies in a thick rough is doubtless a difficult shot to play. But it enables us to understand lag in the golf swing.

Édouard explained that if the action towards the target comes too soon, the grass puts a brake on the club, leading to a fat shot or a top. And he insisted that once again, prediction played a determining role in the natural placement of the body in the "correct" dynamic posture. Cutting the grass under the ball and not at the level of its equator was the "right" command, which once again meant placing one's centre of gravity a little lower than normal.

Sloping ground often creates real difficulties to the extent that it is difficult to practice in such situations. Édouard explained to me that to play successful shots on uneven ground, balance must be maintained for the entire execution of the swing, thereby giving the player perfect control of the trajectory of the ball.

Édouard surprised me yet again since his approach ran counter to conventional teachings. It had been drummed into me that when a ball was higher than one's feet, the body should be aligned well to the right of the flag since the ball would inevitably turn to the left at the end of its trajectory. Almost mechanically. With a ball lower than one's feet however, the body should be aligned well to the left since the ball would inevitably turn to the right at the end of its trajectory.

This was a mistake.

A missed stroke on sloping ground was almost always the result of the body's reaction to a loss of balance and not to incorrect alignment. One should therefore adopt one's usual stance in the same way as when playing strokes with feet on level ground whilst simply taking care to keep one's balance. Sending the ball on all the desired trajectories - fade, draw, low or high, no matter which club was used and whatever the elevation - was within anyone's grasp, provided the "right" setup was initiated and the "right" stance adopted.

Édouard gave me advice for each of the four elevation scenarios that might be encountered on the course.

When the ball is higher than the feet, it is vital to remain centred. The weight is distributed over the balls of the feet. It is essential to avoid reacting to a loss of balance backwards and maintain the centre of gravity perfectly in place during the execution of the swing.

When the ball is lower than the feet, the player should counterbalance the effect of gravity pulling him forwards. The weight of the body transfers naturally to the back of the feet, in the middle of the heels. Gravity places the club nearer the body, contrary to the previous scenario. The shot is therefore played in a more compact manner with both feet remaining perfectly anchored to the ground during the execution of the swing.

When the ball is uphill, Édouard explained to me that particular attention must be paid to balance and centring the swing. Indeed, it was impossible to play this shot in the presence of sway, since the latter led to a lack of balance that was accentuated by the slope. He explained that the challenge here was to position the body perfectly, in the service of the task in hand. In this case, the player should lean on the inside of the right leg to compensate for gravity, which tends to pull the body to the right.

When the ball is downhill, maintaining the head behind during the entire swing is essential. Since gravity pulls the body to the left, the weight naturally falls towards the inside of the left leg. Édouard explained that only the tilt could counterbalance this force.

Like Professor Otto Lidenbrock in his voyage to the centre of the Earth, the apprentice golfer should not be afraid of confronting all the traps and obstacles he meets.

Exploring the element "earth", does not mean plunging in and letting oneself be swallowed up in its depths even though the descent into hell is always latent and threatening.

It means, on the contrary, plumbing all its mysteries. Codes, enigmas, anagrams, and riddles are at the heart of Jules Verne's work.

Travel is always educational.

Indeed, it carries an unexpected message that is disturbing for anyone keen on adventure: however far he travels, Man finds only himself. The exploration of the outer world always melds into that of the inner world.

The extraordinary journey is a journey in the "second degree".

It is a "journey of rediscovery"[113].

It is a formative journey that can change the vision of any apprentice golfer: learning to play *with* oneself and not *against* oneself.

---

[113] In : Mariella di Maio, *Jules Verne et le voyage au second degré ou un avatar d'Edgar Poe (Jules Verne and the Second-degree Journey or an Avatar of Edgar Poe)*, Romantisme, 1990, n°67, Avatars de l'artiste.

EPILOGUE

"...you, who believe I have given a literal account, now, despite yourself, you are a guardian of the Grail".

PÉRONIC

XXVIII.

VALUES IN COMMON WITH COMPANIONS IN THE QUEST

ntor, Galeschin, Gawain, Gaheris, Gareth, Agravain, Bors of Gaunnes, Kay, Ban of Benwick, Lancelot, Galahad, Hector de Maris, Tristan, Mark of Cornwall, Perceval of Wales, Sagramore, Helias, Rience, Claudas, Bagdemagus, the two Ywains, Kahedin, and Dodinel were just a few of the hundred and fifty knights invited to sit at the Round Table set up by Merlin in the Great Hall of Carlisle Castle.

A universal table, round like the world, to which the knights were expected to bring prosperity by putting an end to villainy and injustice. An egalitarian table, that welcomed men of humble birth and around which everyone sat in no hierarchical order. A fraternal table, that exuded an atmosphere of affection and love and which united the knights in shared values and ideals.

Like the hundred and fifty knights carefully selected for their courage, loyalty and fidelity to Arthur, partners in a golf game should also be carefully chosen.

There exist several types of player likely to destabilise the most well-disposed people in the world, delaying their progress. Players who respect neither rules nor etiquette and therefore neither their partners nor the course. Those who cheat, often at the same time exhibiting indexes that have nothing to do with their real level in the game and shamelessly hand in falsified score cards. Those who lie, claiming never to practise, to have only just begun playing yet who are already capable of playing a well-constructed and effective game. Those who act as though they were teachers or commentators or try by every possible means to disturb their partner's concentration and put them off their game. Those who are too slow or too fast. Unfortunately, this list is not exhaustive.

It is vital to choose one's golf partners with great care. The quest for inspired golf is also a quest for integrity. Imposters, liars, cheats, boors, oafs, deceivers, and reprobates have no place here, just as they have no place in the chivalrous world of the Round Table stories.

The exploits and prowess of the knights in Brittany and Great Britain, lands of marvels and enchantment, should not make us forget that chivalry was already highly codified with emblematic values. Generosity, courtesy, magnanimity and selflessness, the chivalric ideal brooked neither compromise nor dishonourable behaviour.

Keeping one's word, observance of the rules of combat, the duty of mercy[114], the requirement to die with honour, fidelity to one's Lady, a whole body of practical common rules was created.

But, above all, *"do not commit any infractions of etiquette"*. These are not the rules of the *Royal and Ancient Golf Club of St Andrews* but the words of Chrétien de Troyes in his admirable poem, *Lancelot ou le Chevalier de la Charrette (Lancelot, or the Knight of the Cart)*[115]. Written more than eight hundred years ago.

---

[114]Consists of granting mercy to a knight one has beaten.
[115]Chrétien de Troyes, *Lancelot ou le Chevalier de La Charrette*, (Lancelot, The Knight of the Cart) *verse 2999*, written between 1176 and 1121.

XXIX.

COMMUNION AND SHARING

Awareness of Man and Planet Earth. Mastery of the self and the five elements. The apprentice golfers can at last enter into communion: communion with the environment, communion with themselves, and with others. Companions in the quest. All those who participate in the search for beauty, integrity, and perfection. All those who pursue the same ideal, share the same values and walk the same path. But not only this.

Whether they are treading the road to success or have wandered from it, whether they have given up or have quite simply not yet undertaken this "adventurous" search, inspired golfers still listen to each person of "good will". Those who have remained sincere, honest, and authentic. Ready to console them. Ready to encourage them. Ready to advise them.

Like Péronic, who when asked about his vocation, said, *"I am pursuing my quest for the Grail, in other words, my quest for love on this Earth, my search for souls with good will"*[116].

The inspired golfer influences those around him. He enlightens others. Communion is, fundamentally, sharing. Sharing of knowledge, apprenticeship, a revelation. But also, and above all, sharing failures, ordeals, discouragement, and fragility.

Communion is a strong desire for alliance, fusion, and closeness. A desire for brotherhood. A desire for humanity. Concern for others.

Like Galahad, the pure Knight, called to sit on the Siege Perilous and who, in the Castle of the Fisher King, simply by asking the injured king about his suffering, independently of his answer, healed him and restored his dignity simply by his thoughtfulness and human compassion. His human compassion, that of pure hearts that are inaccessible to all extraneous preoccupations, and which allow the searcher to reach the Grail.

---

[116]In : Péronic, *Ma Queste du Graal (My Quest for the Grail),* vol.1, Éditions La Pensée solaire, Monte-Carlo, 12 June 1967.

XXX.

THE SYMBOLISM OF THE ROUND TABLE AND THE APPRENTICE GOLFER

The Round Table describes a circle, made up of a centre and radii. The circle corresponds to the complexity of the material journey: Man goes round in circles. The radii correspond to the simplicity of the spiritual journey. They are straight lines that give direct access to the centre. The centre represents the sun, which evokes the first light, the luminous point from which everything proceeds and which the knights in glory sitting round the Round Table contemplate.

The Round Table therefore symbolises the light that guides and inspires the complex, slow, difficult and discouraging journey of all human beings who enter the world, until the enlightenment that permits universal comprehension and which transforms them for ever[117].

In reality, the Round Table describes two circles, one visible, the other invisible, that merge in perfect harmony.

The first circle, which is visible, corresponds to the manifested world. This is the world of the intelligible and temporal. That of reason and technique, which facilitates the acquisition of *skills*.

The second, invisible, circle corresponds to the non-manifested world. It is the world of the non-intelligible, the spiritual. That of sensation and intuition that gives direct access to *knowledge*.

Inspired golf is situated at the point where these two worlds meet and are balanced. Exactly at the crossroads of the tiny space that separates the manifested and the non-manifested, the intelligible and the non-intelligible, the spiritual and the temporal.

This single point that indicates that the two circles are now just one, describes a golf ball.

---

[117]In : *Historique, légende, et symbolisme de la Table Ronde, mythe fondateur de la Chevalerie Spirituelle chrétienne (History, Legend, and Symbolism of the Round Table, Founding Myth of Christian Spiritual Chivalry)*, op.cit.

The Round Table therefore also represents the "philosopher" golf ball. That around which inspired golfers must sit today, like the Knights of King Arthur in the Middle Ages.

Inspired golfers. Those who have managed to execute the perfect movement, who have found the authentic swing.

Those who, in a few fractions of a second, rely at one and the same time and in the same measure, on both skill and knowledge, technique and intuition, reason and sensation.

XXXI.

THE SWORD IN THE ANVIL AND THE CLUB IN THE STONE

xcalibur - or *Escalibor* - is, in popular mythology, the supreme magic sword, the best that has ever been forged. It has extraordinary powers, rejects whoever is not worth of possessing it and is received in a miraculous manner.

It is the sword of truth, of real justice. It is the sword of the chosen one, of King Arthur.

Truth to tell, Arthur had many swords. *Excalibur* and *Marmyadose*, supposedly the sword of Hercules, are the best-known. Stories also mention Caliburn. But they do not all have a name.

Like the sword in the anvil that Arthur extracts by magic on Christmas Eve.

The removal of the sword is loaded with meaning in at least two regards. Firstly, it is an initiation.

Arthur's gesture effects a radical transformation, an irrevocable metamorphosis: the young Arthur becomes king. He therefore attains maturity which means he is autonomous.

Temporal maturity: Arthur is finally ready to unify England and reign. Thanks to an earthly chivalry.

Spiritual maturity: Arthur can found the Round Table, at the instigation of Merlin, and embark on the quest for the Grail. He can found a new chivalric order, a celestial chivalry.

The extraction of the sword is also a rite of passage.

A passage from disorder to order, from an England torn apart and without a king to an England unified and guided by a legitimate king. A passage from apprenticeship as a henchman, to accomplishment as an exemplary sovereign.

The passage from darkness - the young Arthur does not know who his real father is nor the destiny that awaits him – to light – the young king discovers his royal lineage and the work he must accomplish.

This initiation and rite of passage are only possible thanks to the intermediation of a providential person, a temporal and spiritual guide who brings together the non-intelligible and the intelligible, the non-manifested and the manifested, heaven and earth: that of Merlin, a true "archmaster", who takes the young Arthur under his wing from the moment of conception, who teaches him and reveals to him his universal mission.

Merlin, *"the irreplaceable, he whom we wish never to see go but who one day must go,"*[118]. Merlin, whose most characteristic trait is the power of metamorphosis. He who, through magic, transforms a young, illegitimate man into a mythical king.

And the apprentice golfer, into an inspired golfer.

This little work, *"sacred poem, in which heaven and earth have had a hand…*[119]*"*, replaces the sword in the anvil by the golf club in the stone.

And delivers us its secret.

We are all King Arthur. The chosen ones.

It is up to us to remove the club from the stone. Effortlessly. And to play "enchanted" golf. Without stinting.

---

[118]In : René Barjavel, *L'Enchanteur (The Enchanter)*, Éditions Denoël, Paris, 1984.
[119]In : Dante Alighieri, *La Divine Comédie (The Divine Comedy)*, Canto XXV.

"Alchemic golf" that can increase the potential of the light that is in each of us, thanks to finesse and discernment.

Golf "illuminated" by temperance, balance and wisdom. The wisdom that leads to an awakening, to the full realisation of the *self*. And to rapture of the soul. Provided we display consciousness. And mastery. Provided we keep our feet on the ground and our heads in the clouds. And our hearts in the middle.

Inspired golf. The golf of the initiated. That which gives us a glimpse of the Grail.

The Grail, this spiritual hyphen between the heights and the depths, alpha and omega, the uncreated and the created. And above all, between Occident and Orient. Receptacle of the knowledge and consciousness of Universal Man. Over and above churches, mosques, and synagogues. Beyond Shinto sanctuaries, Buddhist temples, Taoïst Palaces and Hindu Mandirs.

The Grail, *"this spontaneous memory of divine things"*[120], *"the face of this God who has no face, who lives only in the hearts of Men"*[121].

The aim of the human adventure.

---

[120]In : Pierre Ponsoye: *L'Islam et le Graal (Islam and the Grail)*, op. cit.
[121]In : André Chouraqui, *Traduire les Textes sacrés (Translating Sacred Texts)*, op.cit.

XXXII.

ETERNITY

olf of Khafre, Giza Plateau, the Left Bank of the Nile, Egypt at dawn, Tee[122] number one, par 5, five hundred and fifty metres, driver in hand.

In front, the majestic Sphinx, seated on the magnetic soil of Egypt, staring impassibly into the Eternity of the Ultimate. In the background, Cheops, eternal pyramid whose expansive point is in tune with the infinite Universe, and then Khafre and Menkaure, the three royal pyramids.

The Nile is several hundred metres away. All around lies the immensity of the desert. The *khamsin*, the hot, dry, and very dusty wind of the south-eastern deserts blows gently. The temperature is already high despite the early hour.

---

[122]Starting area.

I feel these thousand-year old energies deep within me. Time stands still. Faced with the immensity of the desert and the infinite beauty of that space blessed by the gods, I feel the humility and circumspection that are abandonment and letting go. And stepping towards the tee[123], I adopt the words of Amenemope, Pharaoh of the 21st dynasty of Tanis: *"remain humble and circumspect because circumspection is best for the man who seeks perfection"*.

In the distance I can see the Valley Temple, also known as the Low Temple, a place of rebirth that receives the deceased during the funeral ceremony and is a necessary crossing-point towards the eternal home. It was built for the Hereafter, an omnipresent obsession in this unique place.

This entire environment inspires me and elevates me. The manifested world, with its thousand-year old remains that have resisted the ravages of time and the madness of men, and the non-manifested world, that of the Ka, make but one and are but one. They meet at a single point in an exquisite alchemy.

Driver in hand, I am in search of sensation and not key techniques. I feel gravity in the

---

[123]Piece of wood or plastic intended to raise the ball up at the start.

practice swing thanks to perpetual motion, letting the weight of the arm/club unit fall forwards and backwards.

Perfectly centred in the middle of my thoracic cage, at the level of the sternum, whilst I play a practice swing, I feel my body deviate from the path, letting the longest club of my bag calmly complete its cycle to take the ball quite naturally, as it rises again on impact. I feel the right swing and the perfect speed that will allow me to cut the top of my tee, without tension, liberating a maximum of energy.

Totally in connection with my target and with the environment, I give myself up completely to the physical laws of the world that surrounds me. The drive I am preparing to execute whilst I am at address, eyes on the back of the ball, head slightly turned back, is out of my control.

I can see the image. Khafre, my target, in the distance as a backdrop. I prepare to launch my arm/club unit in that direction. No other thought troubles my mind. I am that image. I am Khafre.

Leaning on my left side – I am right-handed -, my feet well planted on the Egyptian earth – I know that power too, comes from the ground -, bathed in these vibrations of eternity, I feel from deep within me the sensation linked to my image.

I am ready. Relaxed, connected, I can now execute the movement I have always known how to do, the movement over which I have instinctive control, despite myself.

The wounds, the suffering, the fits of anger, the doubts that have strewn my path of apprentice golfer are far behind me. Healed and at peace, I measure the distance travelled. Édouard is with me. Shawn too.

In the Khafre golf course, on the Giza Plateau, on the left bank of the Nile, I too am ready to be reborn.

Rebirth. Obligatory crossing point to touch the Universal. And Eternity.

Eternity. The ultimate design.

The same that Virgile the Guide in the *Divine Comedy* tells the Pilgrim Dante when he questions him on the purpose of his journey. "To learn how human beings become eternal "[124].

---

[124]Dante Alighieri, *La Divine Comédie (The Divine Comedy)*, Canto XV.

CONTENTS

Preface

Prologue

THE SECRET OF THE GRAIL AND
THE QUEST FOR INSPIRED GOLF   25

THE CASTLE OF THE GRAIL
AND CASTLES BUILT OF SAND   29

Part One
INITIATION (CONSCIOUSNESS)

THE LONG HARD ROAD   43

OBSCURANTISM   47

DISAPPOINTMENT IN THE
EVERYDAY WORLD   53

FORCES THAT DELAY PROGRESS   57

THE SEARCH FOR "ADVENTURE"   65

THE PROVIDENTIAL MAN   69

THE VERBAL JOUST	71
KNIGHTHOOD	75
THE VISIONARY TROUBADOUR	79
INITIATION	83
THE REVELATION	91
CONSCIOUSNESS OF MAN	97
CONSCIOUSNESS OF PLANET EARTH	103
NON NOBIS	109

Part Two
INSPIRATION (MASTERY)

SALISBURY	121
ENCHANTMENT	125
SENSATION	131
INTUITION	137
MASTERY OF THE SELF	147
MASTERY OF THE FIVE ELEMENTS	151
AETHER	153

FIRE	161
AIR	165
WATER	171
EARTH	175

Epilogue

VALUES IN COMMON WITH COMPANIONS IN THE QUEST	189
COMMUNION AND SHARING	193
THE SYMBOLISM OF THE ROUND TABLE AND THE APPRENTICE GOLFER	195
THE SWORD IN THE ANVIL AND THE CLUB IN THE STONE	199
ETERNITY	205

THE PUPIL (THE AUTHOR)

For many years now, Virgile has worked for the United Nations and in particular, the World Health Organisation. He helps developing countries gradually implement universal health coverage. Enabling the most vulnerable to have access to care and essential health services is his main mission. He is currently working in Madagascar at the service of the Madagascan Ministry of Public Health.

THE MASTER

Édouard has always been passionate about golf and has made it his profession. Since his meeting in 2009 with Shawn, he has disseminated *Wisdom in golf* pedagogy throughout Europe. With more than 7 million views and more than 22,000 subscribers on his YouTube channel, Édouard is now an indispensable reference for learners of golf in all Francophone countries.
www.wisdomingolf.fr

THE FOUNDING FATHER

Shawn is the founding father of *Wisdom in golf*. A former professional player on the Canadian Tour, he has more than 35 years of expertise as an instructor. With more than 44 million views on YouTube and almost 115,000 subscribers, Shawn is one of the most closely followed teachers of golf in the world. Since 2018, he has been Director of development for the *Royal Québec Golf Club and Academy:*
www.wisdomingolf.com